A Woman

and

Her Home

The Best in Wholesome Reading
CHOICE BOOKS Dept. 243
11923 Lee Highway
Fairfax, VA 22030
We Welcome Your Response

A Woman

and

Her Home

Ella May Miller

New Leaf Press

FIRST EDITION
July 1993

Library of Congress Catalog Number: 93-084461
ISBN: 0-89221-241-1

Contents

Preface

I am very aware of the fact that many homemakers today are engaged in activities and in professions outside the home. I am, however, one who firmly believes that the woman who has chosen marriage and family must continue to make that her top priority and not lower homemaking to whatever time is "left over."

God created woman as "mother of mankind" and no one else can take her place. She has been given a sacred privilege and responsibility. In no way do I minimize the importance of husband and father. He is greatly needed and contributes much to the family, but I personally still believe that there is no substitute for a godly wife and mother — one whose life is under the control of her Lord.

Fully aware of a husband and father's importance in the home, I've written this book for the women — the homemakers — who, regardless of their place in society, give this calling top priority. They may be employed outside the home, but are keenly interested in attitudes and relationships which contribute to making their home a positive contribution to society and to God's kingdom.

In this book you will find former "Heart to Heart" radio messages which received wide acceptance from homemakers of the radio audience. Several were previously published in my booklet *Happy Homemaking*. You'll also discover some quotes from years gone by for which I make no apologies. They have stood the test of time.

My prayer is that God will use these pages to help you in solving your daily problems and to bring inspiration for your important task — homemaking.

For happier hearts and homes,
— Ella May Miller

1
The Most Important Career

Why all the controversy about homemaking as an outdated adventure? Don't you know that you're engaged in the most important career in the world? You are! And the most rewarding, too!

With keen interest I've followed Queen Elizabeth's role as homemaker. And from what I glean through newspapers and magazines, the British women love her for her role as wife and mother probably as much as for her position as queen.

And I think many Americans were intensely interested in the late Grace Kelly, the famed actress who *chose* to be a homemaker. After four years of marriage, and two children, a girl, three years and a boy, twenty-two months, Princess Grace made this comment: "I do miss acting, in a way . . . but . . . being married and having children are far more important to me."

Dorothy C. Haskin, also a former actress, says: "I'm a homemaker, and I love it! When I get to heaven, I expect the plaque given to homemakers, because that is where I've wept and prayed and found great joy. Homemaking has been a great adventure to me. I've cooked, sewed, and painted. I've dug in corners, swept ceilings, and enjoyed doing dishes. But only in recent years have I realized that when I cheerfully accepted my job as homemaker, I said, 'Amen!' to the will of God."[1]

I believe God created woman primarily to be a "help-mate" for man (a "helper fit for him," Gen. 2:18; RSV). Together, complementing each other, they as husband and wife would create a "mini-world," a "laboratory of life" where the children they love into existence would learn how to cope with life.

Of course, being a "help-mate" for man reaches beyond the home setting. Women and men work together in the community, in the school, in the church, in the professional world, in culture. Yes, together, in harmonious, cooperative, not competitive, relationships!

To me, being a helper is in no way derogatory. To the contrary, I've always accepted it as a fulfilling, rewarding privilege to be a partner with men in this business of living — beginning in the home. In no way does it express inferiority! (Sinful persons have created that definition. I don't discover it in the Bible.) It's just that God, in His divine wisdom, created male and female to complement each other (not compete with each other), to fill in where one lacks. I've always been elated and excited with the function and role God created for me.

How about the woman who never marries? She also is involved as a homemaker — with a family member, a room-mate(s), or with a parent. So, really, the basic principles and attitudes necessary for rewarding relationships which I portray apply to all women. Each one can transfer these to her own individual situation.

The Bible devotes many passages to this important job. The most familiar one is in Proverbs 31:10-31. I wish you'd read this often and carefully, and if possible, in a modern translation. I guarantee that you'll catch a new vision of your important task.

The Manual Part

Of course, there's the manual part of homemaking. The daily routine chores — getting three nourishing meals, washing dishes, making beds, sweeping, and scrubbing. And it's in this area that many women fail. It's linked to their attitude "I don't like housework." They feel sorry for themselves.

Carrie, at twenty-three, had two small children. The daily routine for a family of four, plus the endless interruptions, "got her down." So she began to escape reality by reading fiction or running over to the next-door neighbors, or talking long hours on the telephone. I don't need to detail the general appearance of her home, of her children, or of the quality of husband-wife relationship.

In contrast, Mary, with three small children, immediately tackled the necessary chores in the morning — dishes, beds, cleaning. Then she'd choose the next important task. She had time to enjoy her children and husband.

The difference between Carrie and Mary was their attitude. Right here lies the secret of success or failure. I'm convinced that life consists mainly of attitudes. These come from within a person — from the heart, the soul, and the mind. That's where God looks when He sees us. That's also what Jesus Christ came into this world to change.

True, our culture has trained us for nearly everything else. We're educated in a masculine world to think masculine. At the same time we are supposed to remain feminine, to retain our softness, our enhancement — the qualities which a husband wants in his wife.

Our "feeling side" gets lost. Caught in the snare of activity, of advancement and material achievement, we lose that "feminine oneness with life" which comes from deep experiences of life, which woman has a unique ability to perceive and pass on to others — bequeathed to her by her Creator. Because of our lack of proper training we assume homemaking to be mediocre, a second or third-rate job. But it isn't!

First a Wife

The wife must be willing to work hard to make a success of her marriage. And here, as in everything else, her attitudes *determine* the result. As the complement to man she fills a unique role. She is queen of her home, he the king. Of course, there is mutual sharing, a desire to please each other, but as wife she will win and maintain his respect through her gentle spirit.

Dr. John A. Schindler says that the woman either makes or breaks her husband. A truck driver, noted for his safe driving, was involved in a highway accident, he at fault. Later questioning by his company officials revealed that just before leaving home that morning he and his wife had a violent quarrel. Many executives today investigate husband-wife relationships before hiring important personnel. Many a man who climbs to the top has a wife who helps boost him.

The wife who truly loves her husband will make

his happiness her primary goal. All loving wives want to please their husbands and create a companionable marriage. This can only be accomplished through the quality of a wife's personal relationship with her husband.

Every husband needs his wife's acceptance, admiration, and appreciation. As she recognizes and fulfills those needs she is encouraging him to give his best to their marriage.

A woman must first be a good wife before she can be a good mother. One marriage counselor advises:

> Remember, you are a wife first, mother second, and if you work, a jobholder third. If you are happy in being a wife, give that role your best. Your job may change, your children may someday be on their own. Where will you be? Unless you want to be on your own . . . then first be a wife.

Happy, harmonious husband-wife relationships — that is the best foundation for happy, well-adjusted children.

Motherhood — A Privilege

One young mother lamented her wasted life — a college education, but now doing nothing but housework and caring for her two small children. In reply, a famous editor told her that her attitude was utter nonsense. In keeping her children on the right road she was as wonderful as a psychiatrist who charges 75 dollars an hour. In decorating her home she was as smart as an interior decorator. And if her family enjoyed eating at home, she was as important as the best chef in a restaurant.

> To be a mother is difficult and danger-
> ous, but no one else can replace her. Will
> women never see how important they are?
> Their power of doing good and doing harm
> is beyond measure, and it is done in private
> where no one can stop them, but themselves.

A mother designs the home. She is by nature the
best equipped to understand, to love, and to teach her
children. Through her daily frequent relationships
with them she guides them into right living. They
observe her example and follow. Right living — coop-
eration, sharing, sacrifice, kindness, and honesty — is
largely caught, not taught. Children need that daily,
close relationship with their mothers. Nothing else
can substitute for this need.

Such relationships give the child security. They
teach him love and how to love others. Dr. John
Bowlby says: "Children must have some one person to
look after them; it must not change every month or
year; child care must have continuity or there is
trouble."[2] Day-nursery care isn't a substitute. "Group
care isn't mothering." He further adds that the child
deprived of a mother's care is anxious and unhappy;
he dreads to be alone — a general feeling of insecurity.

> Some children who have never been
> the objects of continuous care and compan-
> ionship of a single human being, can't love
> and can't learn from experience . . . .
> Deprivation after three isn't quite so
> bad, but it still results too often in excessive
> desires for affection and excessive jealousy,
> which cause acute inner conflict and un-
> happiness . . . . Deprived and unhappy

children are apt to grow up more unstable children.[3]

The mother is the one who brings God and His truths into daily home life. "When the mother of the family forgets God, so does the rest of the family," reads a Navaho proverb.

God has placed into your hands the wonderful privilege of leading your child to know and to love God through Jesus Christ. This is possible as you live like Him, as you connect Him and His ideas with events and questions of the day, as you talk about Him "when you sit in your house, and when you walk by the way . . . lie down, and when you rise" (Deut. 6:7; RSV).

The mother's task is to prepare her child to adjust happily to a larger world — school, community, and church. Of course, she and her husband work together. But because she spends so much time with her child in the formative years, upon her rests the larger share of the responsibility.

Marriage, motherhood, home — the dreams of most young girls. Homemaking should be the most satisfying and most rewarding of all careers. This is the way God planned it to be.

> *Blessed* is she whose daily tasks are a work of love; for her willing hands and happy heart transform duty into joyous service to all her family and God.
>
> *Blessed* is she who opens the door to welcome both stranger and well-loved friend; for gracious hospitality is a test of Christ-like love.
>
> *Blessed* is she who scours and scrubs;

for well she knows that cleanliness is one expression of godliness.

Blessed is she whom children love; for the love of a child is of greater value than fortune or fame.

Blessed is she who sings at her work; for music lightens the heaviest load and brightens the dullest chore.

Blessed is she who dusts away doubt and fear and sweeps out the cobwebs of confusion; for her faith will triumph over all adversity.

Blessed is she who serves laughter and smiles with every meal; for her cheerfulness is an aid to mental and physical digestion.

Blessed is she who introduces Jesus Christ to her children; for godly sons and daughters shall be her reward.

Blessed is she who preserves the sacredness of the Christian home; for hers is a divine trust that crowns her with dignity.

— Adapted by Ella May Miller

2

Marriage Can Be Happy

Bob and Sue had passed through a happy courtship. Then came the wedding, a lovely one.

She had never looked lovelier! Her eyes sparkled, her face radiated happiness.

In front of the church stood Bob — young, stalwart, serious — her ideal.

"Isn't she beautiful!" exclaimed friends with moist eyes. "And they lived happily ever after," predicted another.

Weddings are happy, but as someone has said, the problems come from living together. Bob and Sue are aware of this. How can they remain sweethearts and retain their romance through all their years together?

Problems Will Arise

They enter their marriage, consulting their minds as well as their hearts. They are aware that almost half of all marriages today end in the divorce court. They well know that problems can eat through the lovely fabric of marriage like moths in a silk garment. Psychologists say that finances, sex, religion, children, or in-laws head the list. But are these the real problems?

A Christian psychologist answers,

> Surprisingly enough, those points of trouble are not foremost . . . the crux of marriage difficulties usually stems from the whole human personality. Indeed, *problems of personality cause most marital unhappiness.*[1]

Just as an island in the sea is only a small part of the hidden mountain, so the easily seen problems usually stem from the entire human personality. By the personality we mean the person's total habits, attitudes, and permanent behavior.

Each one of us is different. God didn't cut us from the same pattern.

Now that they are with each other daily, with all masks removed, Bob and Sue are surprised that each has his own way of doing things.

But Bob accepts Sue's personality, her desire to be with people, her easy quips. Sue accepts Bob's slowness, his leaving the clothes on the floor or bed. But she remembers to make over him, not try to make him over.

Bob and Sue try to understand their personality differences and problems. They learn to allow for their personalities and to be tolerant with each other.

Sharing

To accomplish this successfully demands good communications — sharing attitudes, goals, likes, and dislikes. It involves sharing each other on a mental, social, and spiritual level, as well as physical. Doing things together allows for such sharing.

Sue can't continue her social activities as before marriage. Bob can't ignore Sue for his buddies. True, they don't cut themselves off completely from former friends, but they also seek activities of mutual interest.

Sharing means time alone with each other in conversation. Discussion relieves tension. Talking is thinking together. Talking clarifies the solution. Not only are words necessary, but the way they are spoken counts. Bob and Sue are agreeable even though they don't agree at times.

Face Reality

Failure to detect a physical injury can lead to serious consequences. And before the physician can prescribe the proper medication he must diagnose the case.

In marriage the same is true with personality and emotional problems. The couple must face the facts and not run away from them. Bob and Sue are aware of this.

They face the facts. They try to prevent serious problems by taking time to be with each other, time for recreation, for daily sharing and cooperating in the tasks.

Frankness

Bob and Sue are frank with each other. One marriage counselor says that apart from loving each other, complete frankness with each other is the most important factor in a successful marriage.

Too many couples are brutally frank, or they only reveal opinions and attitudes when tense or disgusted. Bob and Sue are kind and considerate of each other with their frankness. Before they retire at night they reveal any wrong attitudes or ill will they have had during the day. They ask forgiveness for unkind words or deeds.

They believe and experience the truth of the Scripture, "If you are angry, don't sin by nursing your grudge. Don't let the sun go down with you still angry — get it over quickly, for when you are angry you give a mighty foothold to the devil" (Eph. 4:26-27;LB).

Unselfishness

Sue *wants* to keep her marriage happy. She unselfishly lives for Bob's happiness, and to create a warm, happy home atmosphere he will enjoy and want to come home to. Her loyalty is to him. Bob is considerate of Sue's wishes, and together they agree concerning the spending of money and time, concerning the daily activities. They *want* to remain sweethearts.

Love Gives, Not Demands

Bob and Sue continue to express their love in daily, thoughtful gestures and deeds — a thank you for the delicious meal, for a cozy home, for the fix-it jobs. They remember birthdays and anniversaries.

Tell Her So

Amid the cares of married life,
In spite of toil and business strife,
If you value your sweet wife,
Tell her so!

There was a time you thought it bliss
To get the favor of a kiss;
A dozen now won't come amiss —
Tell her so!

Don't act as if she's past her prime,
As though to please her were a crime
If e'er you loved her, now's the time;
Tell her so!

You are hers and hers alone;
Well you know she's all your own;
Don't wait to carve it on the stone —
Tell her so!

Never let her heart grow cold,
Richer beauties will unfold,
She is worth her weight in gold;
Tell her so!
    — Mrs. John H. Whipple

When couples drift apart, whether in the first or twentieth year of marriage, the most likely cause is they have failed to express their love for each other in daily words and acts.

Learn to Love
Even couples who may have had little love at marriage can learn to love each other. They can develop the perfect love that casts out fear.

One wife says,

> Our marriage was about to break up. I didn't love John. But one day I let Jesus take over my life. I began to ask, "How would I act if I did love my husband?" Then I consciously began learning his likes and dislikes. I prepared his favorite dishes. I joined in his hobbies. I bought surprises to put in his lunch at noon. Now I love him with all my heart. But my greatest reward came the other day when our teenager said,

"Mom, I'm lucky."

"Oh," I answered. "Why?"

"You and Dad love each other. You'd be surprised how many kids have parents who fight and quarrel most of the time."

Faith

Another ingredient in a happy marriage is faith in God as Saviour, who removes all guilt, who lifts you up when you fall, and gives you a new start. Faith in the One who alone can give you daily courage, contentment, joy, and peace, regardless of circumstance. Faith in God, the source of truth, love, and lasting values.

Learn to accept each other. Live for each other unselfishly. Face the facts. Take time to talk frankly together and to be with each other. Daily show love. Have a practical faith in Almighty God. Your marriage can be happy!

Continued Courtship

Happy is the family (couple)
In which the ways of courtship
Are not forgotten nor abandoned,
But continued through the years.

For though love is a plant from heaven
It grows best on earth when most cultivated,
And being cultivated and tended,
It puts forth new roots and branches
And fresh leaves and flowers.

It bears pleasant and abundant fruit
In all months of the year,
And its fruit is for those two
Who cultivate the plant together.[2]

3

Why Worry?

Someone may answer, "If I don't do the worrying around here, no one else will!"
Here's one mother's situation:

> I'm desperate . . . . For eight years we've been engaged in a desperate financial struggle. In order to keep our farm home, we were forced to expand our business and this made it necessary for my husband to find outside employment in addition to farming. For six years now he has worked eight hours a day in a factory and then tries to farm 120 acres at night. I'm left alone with the children five days a week with no transportation, and my husband sees us for about one-half hour a day.
>
> I have a heart condition which forces me to spend much of my time in resting. My husband has no time to help me around the house. We cannot afford hired help for either of us. My family lives thousands of miles away. I cannot stand the strain much

longer and my health is breaking because
of it.

Isn't this desperate mother justified in worrying?

Big and Little Problems

Many wives and mothers have terrific problems.
There are smaller problems that confront each one of
us daily. Will the children be safe walking to school?
There might be an accident on the playground or at
work. One mother calls at her son's place of employ-
ment every time an ambulance passes her house,
fearful he's been involved in a serious accident.

When traveling, some people are on edge, fearful
that the other driver might lose control of his car and
involve them in a wreck. People worry today because
they can't buy everything they want. Some worry
about losing their jobs, or about death. You name it! In
any area, worry or overanxiety is possible. And far too
many people today are guilty of indulging in this evil.

Think of the problems that tend to overly concern
you. Have you solved your problem, be it small or
large, through worrying? An honest answer can only
be no. Someone has said, "Worry is like a rocking
chair. You're doing something, but getting nowhere."

A young Indian lad saw a white man
running down the road and asked his
grandmother why the man ran. "Because,"
said the old woman, "the man does not
know that the road has no end."
We might all of us worry less if we had
the wisdom of this old Indian woman.[1]

"Worry is a circle of inefficient thought whirling

about a pivot of fear," says Dr. Robert B. Martin.

Results of Worry

It's true, worry is inefficient thought getting you nowhere. There's another sense in which this is wrong. Worry does get you somewhere! Into trouble! Into the doctor's office! Into bed! Or into your coffin!

"Worry often gives a small thing a big shadow."

I honestly believe that worrying about accidents was the mother of insurance agencies. Let me illustrate. I was told of a young father who was afraid he might be injured or killed, so he obtained an expensive life insurance policy. Next he secured the most complete coverage in car insurance, and then insured his home. And at the time his cousin told me about his dilemma, he had just taken out expensive insurance covering his children at school. His cousin concluded, "Now he's almost frantic worrying about meeting his payments."

Don't tell me worry doesn't get you anywhere!

There are young couples who are overly concerned about their reputation in their circle of friends. To make an impression they buy a new car, the latest furniture, the latest fashion in clothes — all on installment buying, and are driven frantic trying to meet monthly payments.

And mothers are often guilty of worrying about their children's future, their achievements, their popularity, their vocation. In fact, they worry to such extremes that they completely ruin their chances for normal living.

Causes Illness

Worry not only gets you into a mess, into more trouble socially and mentally, it affects you physically.

Dr. Charles Mayo says: "Worry affects the circulation, the heart, the glands, the whole nervous system, and profoundly affects the health. I have never known a man who died from overwork, but many who died from doubt."[1]

The woman whose letter I quoted earlier confessed to illness and to nervousness.

> A large industrial concern discovered that nine out of ten cases of workers' inefficiency were caused by worry. A life insurance company found that four out of five nervous breakdowns began not in actual events but in worry. A medical clinic's analysis of its patients showed that 35 percent of all illnesses on its records started with worry.[2]

Worry drains the body of its energy and powers. It confuses issues, creates frustration and tension. And the tragic truth is that most worrying is done about things that won't or don't ever happen! It's wise not to cross the bridge until you get there.

Lack of Faith

There's also a spiritual facet connected with worrying. "If you trust you do not worry; if you worry you do not trust." This is so true! Worry is sin. Its root is doubt. The mother I quoted in the beginning of this chapter added, "I know it's a sin to worry, but . . . ."

You're no doubt familiar with this verse:

> Said the robin to the sparrow,
> "I should really like to know
> Why these anxious human beings
> Rush about and worry so."

Said the sparrow to the robin,
"Friend, I think that it must be
That they have no heavenly Father
such as cares for you and me."
                — Elizabeth Cheney

There's only one cause for real worry. That is if you're still carrying all the weight of sin and guilt on your own shoulders. But in this also you can find peace and rest as you apply Christ's cleansing power.

Remedy for Worry

To know God is to know peace of mind. To be personally acquainted with Him and His promises eliminates worry. He who created everything out of nothing and who controls all things is interested in you. With Him "nothing is impossible." Or, in a positive statement, "All things are possible" with Him.

He tells us that He notes the sparrow's fall. The very hairs of your heard are numbered. One who interests himself in such trivia surely cares about your concerns — personal ones such as your marriage, your family, or financial problems. In fact, He is interested and has made provision for you so that you don't need to be overly concerned.

One of my favorite Bible passages is Matthew 6:25-34, where Jesus tells of God's concern about birds and flowers, and about each individual. He concludes:

Set your heart on his kingdom and his goodness, and all these things will come to you as a matter of course. Don't worry at all then about tomorrow. Tomorrow can take care of itself! One day's trouble is enough for one day (Matt. 6:33-34;Phillips).

If you love God with all your heart and are living out His ideas in your life, why worry about food and clothes? This promise "All these things will come to you as a matter of course" is like a blank check. Fill in and sign your name when you need it! Remember, you can cash it only for *needs*, not for wants!

I've used this promise ever since I was a teenager working my way through school. It has never failed. Naturally, I've never folded my hands and expected the dollar bills to fall out of the sky. Quite the contrary. I've worked whenever necessary. Yet, God was back of the jobs.

Life is more than money, more than many and costly clothes. Life is more than rich foods and desserts, more than fame. Life is peace and joy, and love which shows itself in living for others and helping them.

And if, after carefully observing health rules, sickness comes, or if accidents occur, we can claim this promise: "All things work together for good to them that love God" (Rom. 8:28).

"God is still on the throne; He never forsakes His own."

> Don't worry over anything whatever; tell God every detail of your needs in earnest and thankful prayer, and the peace of God, which transcends human understanding, will keep constant guard over your hearts and minds as they rest in Christ Jesus (Phil. 4:6-7;Phillips).

4

Effective Discipline

A newspaper editor arrived home one evening, kissed his wife, and asked, "Well, how was everything today?"

"Pretty good," came her reply. "The latest issue of *Parents' Magazine* was a big help, though, straightening out our dear little daughters who were acting up."

"Good. What was the article?"

"No article. I just rolled up the magazine and gave them a good shellacking."

Sometimes discipline does need to be in the form of spanking, but it should be left for rare occasions; if not, it will become too common, and mean absolutely nothing. And, as in the above illustration, it's good for both parents to be united, to uphold each other's method of discipline.

Firm Discipline

Some parents are hesitant to be firm with their child, fearful that he will lose his respect for them or fail to love them. But interestingly — the opposite is true. Firm discipline, given in love and fairness, creates love and respect in the child.

Discipline means "teaching." And to get your point across you use methods that cause the child to understand your words and your rules.

Conrad Jensen, a high-ranking police officer in New York City, says that parents of young lawbreakers have most harmfully failed their children in this area. According to him, "The attitude of children toward their parents reveals no discipline."

Of his own home, policeman Jensen says,

> I would tolerate no disobedience . . . . Punishment should be given calmly, but even the kids forgave me when I did it in temper. A few times I punished when they hadn't done wrong and I asked their forgiveness . . . . The Lord has given us two wonderful grown-up children, in spite of the mistakes we made.[1]

Jensen contends that the greatest factor causing so many crimes is that youngsters have no fear of punishment. They know no discipline, and think they can get by.

I'm grateful that, as parents, we can look to God for guidance. He who created human nature knows how it can be guided and directed. In His Holy Word I read, "The rod and reproof give wisdom: but a child left to himself bringeth his mother to shame . . . . Correct thy son, and he shall give thee rest; yea, he shall give delight unto thy soul" (Prov. 29:15,17).

Indeed, firm discipline, given in love and with reason, does help a child to learn what is right.

Self-discipline
When parents learn self-discipline, they will have

fewer problems with the child.

There are reasons behind a child's behavior. As you look for causes of unacceptable behavior, take a look at yourself. Are you tired, irritable, on edge? These emotional strains are catching. If you are feeling happy and relaxed, you will have very few problems with your child. However, when you do need to punish, quietly explain your reason for it.

Back of your discipline is the idea of teaching the child self-discipline. As he grows older he'll learn to control himself without his parents' continual aid. This calls for much wisdom and patience on your part. As you discipline your child ask yourself, "Is this helping him establish standards of acceptable conduct? Does this encourage and show him how to control himself?" If so, you are disciplining wisely.

A United Front

Parents teach best *together*. They need to discipline together. The child needs a father and a mother, but they should be united. When one parent joins with the child against the other, this creates emotional conflicts in themselves as well as in the child. It causes frustration, guilt, and instability.

Dr. David R. Mace, marriage counselor, says that it is a dangerous position for parents to adopt different policies. This then gives the child a golden opportunity to play off one parent against the other. Furthermore, in so doing he loses respect for them.

Parents should agree upon the rules the child must learn to respect. They should present a solid and united front. All parents do have some differences of opinions, but their differences should be discussed and resolved out of his hearing. They need to support each other.

Marital Conflicts

Parents who hold different theories on child raising usually have marital conflicts, and the child is used by them as a battleground. They are hitting at each other through him.

Parents who enjoy warm relationships with each other will share them with their child. Dad is as eager that the child love his mother as he is that the child loves him. He'll avoid any situation to belittle her in his eyes. This holds for mother, too.

Without warm relationships between mother and father, they can't act as a team. Their approach to the child will reproduce their unresolved conflicts.

Several years ago a heartbroken mother wrote the touching story of her son, a dangerous criminal. In her summary she says that first and foremost, he was reared in a broken home. True, the parents were living together, but *they were divided*. They did not present a united front in training their son. He then learned to exploit the situation and profit through dishonesty and deceit.

Creates Emotional Problems

According to psychiatrists there are many children with severe emotional conflicts caused by this same condition. They have been the football for the parents' marital conflicts.

But what if one parent knows his decision is right, the other definitely wrong? This may, and does, present a problem, especially in today's culture with the father away from home much of the time. He probably appears on the scene a short while in the evening. Then very frequently, too preoccupied with his newspaper or books, he is unaware of the total picture.

On the spur of the moment he may make an

unwise move. But even here, rather than cross him in front of the children, mother and he should discuss it calmly and frankly when alone. Mother may make wrong decisions, too. If a parent makes a wrong decision, he should apologize to the child. This, in the total picture, is better than one parent taking issue with the other.

I recall Dr. Mace's statement: "Parenthood is complicated and to be effective it must be a cooperative task. The degree of success achieved by a couple as parents is determined by the degree of success which they can achieve in marriage."[2]

Your child is not a football to be kicked about by marital disharmony. He will suffer all his life from insecurity and emotional problems. Ask God to help you settle your differences alone, and then present a united front to your child. He needs two parents, but "the two shall be one."

Guiding Principles for Effective Discipline

1. *Parents should say what they mean* and then stick to it. This implies deliberation before arriving at a decision. If you tell Junior to be home ten minutes after school is dismissed, see that he does it. If you give a decision and later realize it wasn't the wisest, in most cases it is best to follow through with it. However, at times additional information or changing circumstances will necessitate a change in decision. In these cases the child should be told exactly why you are changing your mind.

2. *There must be consistency.* You can't allow one thing today when you're feeling fine and tomorrow forbid it because you're tired and crabby.

3. *Either forgive or punish an offense; never threaten.* This is an enforced rule in Chinese homes. Their

children are very obedient and courteous. And there's no need for me to go into detail — you and I know what usually happens to threats — they're forgotten (by the parents) or continually repeated, but never fulfilled.

4. *Both father and mother must agree* to uphold each other's decisions and commands. However, should different opinions exist, they should be discussed privately.

5. *Firm discipline must be accompanied by warm love,* lots of fun, and kindness. Don't retain an ill feeling or grudge against children. Follow God's rule — to *forget* after the act is dealt with.

6. *Always keep in mind that discipline is for the child's good.* For example, to punish a child unkindly for accidentally spilling the milk isn't discipline. It's giving vent to your feelings. However, deliberate disobedience, lack of respect, and planned destruction on the child's part need to be dealt with.

7. *We parents must have some kind of chart or goals,* either mentally or written, to be able to evaluate properly the child's actions in light of long-range character. We must know which traits to develop and which ones to nip. We must then know how to go about encouraging the favorite ones and curbing the undesirable ones.

8. *We must really believe that rules and limits are necessary.* God's universe is run with rules. The earth doesn't one day decide to quit revolving on its axis, or stop for one hour when it feels like it. According to scientists, scientific formulas and equations are fixed. Because they do not vary *Columbia* could repeatedly be launched into orbit, collect data about outer space, and re-enter the earth.

9. *Effective discipline requires much time,* much thought, much patience, and much prayer. To let the

children do as they please is to follow the path of least resistance. Older children need careful teaching and explanations as to why we believe and act as we do. And we need a power beyond our puny selves to be able to stand against the strong current of "everybody else does it."

10. *We must be examples* by our submission to God's order and rules for our own happy, contented, and successful living. And I firmly believe that discipline in the home is the only road that leads a child to submission to outside authority — the school, the state, the church — and ultimately submission and obedience to God.

This is a big order, isn't it? But if we want happy, contented, and acceptable children we must sacrifice to achieve these goals, and God is very willing to help us.

Children Want Discipline

Of course, children aren't aware that they want discipline, nor do they usually ask for it, but they do want it. Take the case of four-year-old Nan who whined and fussed all morning long. Mother's suggestions to color in her new book, to play with the dolls, or to have a tea party were all thrown aside. And against her mother's threats, she repeatedly opened the oven door to peep at the cake. Finally, in desperation her mother jerked Nan from the floor, slapped her smartly, and laid her on the bed. To her astonishment Nan sobbed, "I wish Daddy were home. He'd make me listen." Nan appreciated Daddy telling her what she could do and what she couldn't do. All children appreciate that because children do want discipline!

The Bible says, "He who loves him [his son] is diligent to discipline him" (Prov. 13:24;RSV); and

"Discipline our son, and he will give you rest; he will give delight to your heart" (Prov. 29:17;RSV).

5

Money and Things

Regardless of age or income, we all battle constantly with this issue: materialism — money and things.

And I'm wondering if perhaps we carry about in our minds the wrong concept of wealth. This can be true whether we belong to a group desiring riches or to the group who already possesses it. Is wealth necessary for a smooth and contented happy home and family relationships?

In my close observation of happy, contented living, I'm forced to conclude that the gift of happiness and contentment is not dependent on the family's income. And quite frequently, it's the reverse from what most people think.

The Abundance of Things

I don't believe people in any country or in any age have been surrounded with the terrific temptation to make more money and to possess so much more as we are. The comparative ease with which we can earn money! The multitudes of things surrounding us!

When they were young, my daughter and youngest son went with me one day to shop for school clothes. As we walked up one aisle and down the other Jeanne would motion to me, "Oh, Mother, look at this doll set! Can't I have it?" or, "Buy some candy."

To these remarks I replied calmly, "No."

"Well, why not? Just 39 cents a pound. The doll costs only $2.98. I have some money in my purse. I can get it." And then — well, you probably can imagine the resulting scene as I insisted we needed all the money for clothes.

My son wasn't interested in candy and dolls. He pulled toward the balls, gloves, and boots. So many things to desire! Such enticing displays! And comparatively reasonable in price!

Money and things! Both necessary! Both needful in living a normal life. In days of old the barter system served as a medium of exchange. Today money is primarily that commodity which we all need to have as an exchange for that which we don't have.

Money is necessary! But it can become your master. You can become its slave.

Wealth Can't Buy Happy Home Relationships

Father and mother work daily from early till late and neglect their natural and spiritual obligations to their children. Parents supply children with things, with material comfort, and many extras which they wish. Parents provide possessions instead of companionship, counsel, guidance, teaching, and relationships — just themselves.

Years ago I met a fine family. The father was ambitious. Money came easily. He became so intrigued with it that he expanded his business — so much that soon he spent his time only as the boss. Employees did the work. His sons helped at times. But soon they were gone, lost to him and to God. He had no time with them except in businesslike relationships or to give them material needs. No working together. No companionship. No time for fishing, for picnics, for relaxation. If so, he would have lost some "deals!" His income would have been reduced!

And not only are fathers guilty. Far too many mothers today covetously eye the glittering apple of money. They feel it, smell it, fondle it, and soon, like Eve, yield to its alluring charms. And if they are honest they awake too late, like Eve, with the realization that they have forfeited real life. They have forfeited happy, contented living both for themselves and for their family. They have sacrificed their sons and daughters on the altar of money. They fail to realize that "all that glitters is not gold."

Too frequently married couples choose wealth or a new house or a new car instead of children! How foolish! They don't know what they're missing. No amount of money can reward parents as can the love and devotion of children.

Bound to money, like Siamese twins, are "things."

Like my daughter and son, mothers can get captivated with the lovely displays in the stores. They lose their sense of values and needs, and succumb to satisfying wants that could be denied and yet not hinder happy living. Years ago I visited in a home that actually resembled a discount store. The mother could not resist the "lust of the eye." So on each shopping tour she returned home loaded with unnecessary bowls, dishes, vases, ceramics, and little gadgets which eventually filled her cupboards. Others found a nesting place in the attic.

Of course, she didn't invest in evil or sinful things. But they were quite unnecessary to happy living.

Who Gives Wealth?

I'd like to ask some questions. Do you think it is wrong to buy unnecessarily and luxuriously when more than half this world's peoples have no homes? When an equal amount go to bed nightly with hungry, gnawing stomachs? Aren't we responsible to God for the 90 percent we keep as well as for the 10 percent we give back to Him?

You may retort, "I guess I worked hard for every penny I've earned. It's my business how I spend it!"

After all, you must admit that unless God had endowed you with healthy mental and physical capacities you could not earn one penny. And I'm quite certain that He expects us who are industrious and have money above our needs to share with others. Yes, He allows us to earn, but surely He anticipates honesty, generosity, and unselfishness as guiding principles — always. While many condemn needless spending as a sin, they seem unaware that keeping all their money for themselves while others are in need is just as sinful in God's sight.

Love of Money

The Bible says, "The love of money is the root of all evil." As we examine today's American life we can well ask, "Why distill millions of gallons of alcoholic beverages yearly? Why manufacture tons of cigarettes? Why print ninety million comic books monthly? Why produce sexy, immoral shows? Why sell drugs? Why sell millions of pieces of pornographic literature yearly? Why? Why?" You know the answer. Certainly not to produce pure, clean, upright character in our two hundred fifty million Americans. Certainly not to help them to know God, their Creator, and the Ruler of all the earth. No, these are purely lucrative businesses.

Right Attitudes toward Money

It's up to parents to develop right attitudes toward money and things in their children. Be examples as parents who use money as an exchange for that which is needful. Don't be its slave. "You can't serve God and mammon (money)." It's either one or the other. Show your children that money ill-gained, through deceit or dishonest methods, or by taking advantage of the ignorant or poor, is not worth it!

Show them examples of generosity and helpfulness. Let them cooperate and share in the family expenses. I believe that children learn more effectively in this method than by keeping everything they earn. The latter method creates an independent spirit and an uncooperative attitude.

One family has arrived at this pattern. The parents allow their young children 2 percent of their individual earnings, but the rest goes toward family living. They keep "tips" given in their various jobs. They also receive surprise awards occasionally from the parents. The children are happy in this sharing project.

Just another observation — children with too much money jingling in their pockets are gullible targets for pornographic literature, immoral shows, excessive sweets, gadgets, cigarettes, liquor, and drugs.

Money Versus God

The Word of God has much to say about money, about wealth. In the Old Testament God repeatedly warned the children of Israel that after they entered the Promised Land, after they had wealth and possessions, they should beware lest they forget Him — the Giver of everything.

You know the result. They were a prosperous

people. But they forgot God. And yet they didn't have to forget Him.

There are prosperous individuals who have retained a sane balance of living, who have not forgotten God. I think they have caught the biblical philosophy or attitude toward money and possessions:

> Give me neither poverty nor riches; feed me with the food that is needful for me, lest I be full, and deny thee, and say, "Who is the Lord?" or lest I be poor, and steal, and profane the name of my God (Prov. 30:8-9;RSV).

> There is great gain in godliness with contentment; for we brought nothing into the world, and we cannot take anything out of the world; but if we have food and clothing, with these we shall be content (1 Tim. 6:6-8;RSV).

The rich in this world should not set their hopes on uncertain riches but on God who richly furnishes us with everything to enjoy. "They are to do good, to be rich in good deeds, liberal and generous" (1 Tim. 6:18;RSV). In this way they lay up treasures in heaven. There no one robs or steals their riches. There is no inflation or swindling.

You see, "A man's life [a woman's life, or a child's life] does not consist in the abundance of his possessions" (Luke 12:15;RSV).

Let's question ourselves honestly before we buy: "Do I need this dress? Do I need this new furniture? Do we need a new home? Do we need a new car?"

Don't try to keep up with the Joneses. Keep happy

and contented within your circumstances. Resolve to live above things for, after all, they wear out, rust, and break. The children will forget what you possessed materially, but happy and contented attitudes, a love for God and for people, will stay with them eternally.

Let money and things serve you. Don't become their slave.

6

How to Handle Fear

Many people suffer from fear. Unrelieved fear is damaging to the mind and body. It causes torment — mental anguish, real pain, and suffering.

Fear produces physical symptoms — upset stomach, headaches, nervousness, and other ailments.

Fear silently robs people of good health and happiness. In fifty out of every hundred people, vision is impaired when they are even slightly frightened. Fear can cause your thought processes to practically stop; you "freeze in your tracks." You can't think clearly and rationally as before. So you shouldn't tackle a tough problem or make decisions when you are fearful.

Parents who use fear to discipline their children actually defeat their purpose. This sets up mental blocks hindering the learning process or causes the child to "clam up," forgetting that which he already knew. Fear clogs his ability to think. It's a form of mild panic and discourages learning.

God says, "Fear has torment." It's a devastating thing. We do not want to be guilty of creating fear in our children's hearts and lives.

How Fear Begins

How does fear begin? From training, or through experience? The answer is *both*. And whether we realize it or not, as parents we reflect our fears in our actions and reactions. We impose them on our children.

Phyllis, for example, was terrified by electrical storms. In her childhood whenever a thunderstorm came up, her mother would grab Phyllis and her sister and rush them into a closet. There they tremblingly huddled together until the storm passed.

People also develop fears because they have been frightened. Fear may be a result of a series of experiences in early years causing maladjustments in later life, especially if there is no self-confidence.

June is an example of the latter type. Her difficulty didn't show up until she was married. She was afraid to entertain guests. She lacked the confidence in her ability to cook or properly serve guests in her home. Why? June's mother had never allowed her to help in the kitchen. The few times she did try cooking ended in failure and the family laughed at her. So, you see June was *afraid* to try.

Fear Instilled

Some mothers are always worrying about the child's health. One mother, without fail, took her children's temperature every morning. At the slightest irregularity she would question, "Does your head hurt? Are you sick to your stomach?" Her children enjoyed many days at home from school because she *made* them sick. They had not complained or thought of any sickness before her probing.

Harsh, stern parents or divorce in a family implants uncertainty, resentment, or fear in a child's mind. He loses respect as well as a sense of security and stability of *anything* in the world.

As mothers we can do much to keep our children from developing fears by not using *fear* as a means of discipline. The *fear* method is not only unsound, it's unkind! "Now you eat your cereal or the bogeyman will get you." "Stay out of the street or the policeman will grab you." "I'll put you in that dark closet." Such threats may bring quick results, but they also may cause emotional damage that will leave a permanent scar.

It's much better to spank a child or take away some privileges than to hold the weapon of fear over his head.

We also want to teach children to respect common dangers such as electric fans, matches, or hot stoves. But we should do all in our power to prevent them from being unduly fearful. Combined with precaution is a confidence that one can meet whatever life may bring.

Understanding Minimizes Fear

We seldom fear the things we understand. That's why it's so important for parents to talk to children about their fears. When Beth was a small child the trees on her street dropped strange reddish blossoms. To her they were worms and she recoiled at the sight of them. But when her mother discovered her fears, she told Beth that they were blossoms and not worms. They preceded the leaves and soon the tree would be dressed in its lovely green robe. She then laid a blossom in her hand and described its beauty. Beth didn't *like* the blossoms but she was no longer afraid of them.

Preparation Reduces Fear

People are also fearful of the unknown. We should

prepare our children to accept new experiences rather than to fear them.

Mother accompanied Jimmy to school on his first day. He tightly held her hand and cried, "Don't go away, Mommy." To calm him she promised that she wouldn't leave. But the moment the teacher had Jimmy's eye, Mother slipped away. Well, you know what happened the next morning. Jimmy had two fears instead of one — the fear of a new situation (the classroom) and the fear that his mother wouldn't keep her word.

Most children are afraid of new experiences. But you can never solve the problem by deceit. *Talk* with your children. *Explain* just what to expect. Then be sweetly firm — *always* honest.

Wrong Methods

Teasing and ridicule don't help a fearful person. Neither can you force a frightened person.

Diane feared feathers. Her brothers thought that this was silly. They laughed and teased about it, but Diane continued to be afraid. One day they decided to cure her. The boys hid behind the front door and as Diane entered the house they showered her with feathers from a pillow. Diane went into hysterics. Nothing that the boys or her parents could do calmed her. They summoned a physician who diagnosed it as a severe case of shock. It was several days before she was well enough to sit up in bed. Besides the physical damage was the emotional damage. Today, as a grown woman, Diane still breaks out in a cold sweat whenever she sees a feather. Confidence in her brothers and the whole world was shattered that day. As a result she has a restricted, fearful personality — simply because someone wanted to force her out of her fear.

Another foolish way to handle fear is simply to say, "Relax." Merely telling a person to relax is not the solution. But talking it out with a sympathetic friend does help.

Children cannot overcome fears simply by ignoring them. Take the case of Timmy. Timmy was afraid of the dark. His mother said, "How silly! A big boy like you! I'm ashamed of you!" Then she snapped off the light and walked out of the room. Timmy buried his head under the covers and began to sob. Timmy continued to hate bedtime!

Susan's mother discovered that her daughter was afraid of the dark. So, she put a little nightlight in her room. She often sat on her bed and talked to her, "Everything is all right, honey. Mother and Daddy are right here in the next room. We'll leave the door open, and you can call us if necessary. But better than that, Jesus is right here with you. He loves you, we all love you, and we're going to take care of you." Susan learned to combat fear with confidence.

Condition with Confidence

A mature attitude recognizes that certain dangers — car accidents, fires, ill health — do exist, and then proceeds to take preventative measures. Parents teach children best by their own exemplary, mature attitudes toward calamities or disasters. They discuss such events in a constructive way, not whining or griping.

Parents can set a tone of cheerfulness, of looking on the bright side, for the whole family, which carries them through the whole day.

They must keep alert to the child's reaction to such incidents as an actual robbery in the community. They can explain that this is uncommon. Their own lack of fear of robbers in their own home will go a long way to give the child an attitude of courage.

An excellent way to develop mature attitudes in the family is group reading around the table or in the living room. This way parents can comment on events, or on the children's remarks, and instill an attitude of courage.

In addition to these methods Christian parents will give to their children the promises of God — that He will be with us *always* and protect us. When a man's heart is right with God, he makes even his enemies to be at peace with him. There is the other side, too. Should cause for fear arise, we *know* God doesn't forget us, even for one moment. He'll order all things for our good. Such confidence motivates courage in the face of alarm.

The child can be taught not to fear death. Death is a necessary part of living. It's to be expected. Wise parents will refer to death as a natural event. They won't shield the child from it, but will comment on its meaning as he faces it from time to time. In this area we Christians are at an advantage. Death for us is a long-anticipated event — the time when we step across the threshold from the unpleasantries of earthly living to eternal happiness.

How to Overcome Fear

What if you are fearful? Can you be freed from such a binding chain? It will first be necessary to see exactly what you *fear* and what the *fear is*.

Grace was continually scrubbing and fumigating her home, and avoiding people with multiple sclerosis, fearful she would get the disease. When told it was not contagious, her fears remained. As she analyzed the cause, she remembered sitting beside a victim of multiple sclerosis at a church supper. She helped clean up the mess caused by his dropping food on the table and floor. Later that evening she spilled some food.

Grace was aware how her fear began. Now she needed to know what the fear was. Whenever she saw a multiple sclerosis patient her heart began pounding loudly, her hands trembled, and she experienced difficulty in breathing. Fear itself is a physical state that has been cross-conditioned to certain things. Once fear is established, it isn't just a notion; it's an emotion.

To recondition your fear dig up the cause, realize it's a physical state, then remember these physical symptoms are automatically produced by a conditioning factor. Tell yourself not to be afraid of the emotional reaction. Also, expose yourself to that which brings on the fear, all the while telling yourself, "I can lick this thing."

Faith

Human techniques aren't enough to banish fear. Only God understands our basic needs and He helps us to meet them in ways superior to man's.

God promises never to leave us nor forsake us: "Fear thou not; for I am with thee . . . for I am thy God: I will strengthen thee" (Isa. 41:10). He doesn't promise escape from every fearful situation, but He does promise to walk with you through each experience. As you keep close to Him you can be strong and unafraid with Him, the strength of your life.

Even then, there are some Christians who have fears because they start losing fellowship with God. Fear does not come from God. God is love and "there is no fear in love," the Bible says. But the way back to peace of mind is through confessing the things that make one fearful and anxious, turning to Christ and walking close to Him daily. Only this will make one free from worry and fear.

I'd like to paraphrase a Bible verse to read: "Don't be afraid of *anything,* but with thanksgiving, frequently discuss *everything* with God. And His peace, which passes *all* logical reasoning or understanding, *will* keep your mind free from fear in Christ Jesus" (Phil. 4:6-7;free trans.).

If you don't know God as your Saviour from sin and as your best Friend, you have plenty to be afraid of! Both in this life and in the life to come!

As you trust Christ and depend on Him you can say, "God hath not given us [me] the spirit of fear; but of power, and of love, and of a sound mind" (2 Tim. 1:7).[1]

7

Mental Health

During this week approximately thirty million Americans, nearly 12 percent of the population, will consult a physician. Yet, despite their aches and pains, more than half of these will have no diagnosable physical ailment. What's their trouble? They are afflicted with illnesses of mental or emotional origin.

Dr. Philippe Cardon, Jr., internist at the National Institute of Mental Health, Bethesda, Maryland, says that the large majority are "unhappy people whose lives aren't going well, and just don't feel good."

Millions of people yearly receive some treatment in mental hospitals, and many others with less acute illnesses manage to stay away.

Mental health, emotional health, is a subject of vital interest to us as mothers and homemakers.

A Personal Thing

What is mental health? I hesitate to define it, for mental health is a highly personal thing. It differs for each individual. There are no simple, easy answers.

However, we do judge it by our behavior patterns which act as barometers reflecting our inner pressures. And behavior is only the outward reflection of our mental, emotional, moral, and spiritual state. It is a result of our attitudes toward ourselves, toward other people, toward our environment, and toward God. It is a continual process of making adjustments, of adapting ourselves to the experiences of the daily activities of life.

Mental health is of great importance to us as mothers, because we spend much time with and are very closely bonded to the child in those early formative years of his life. It is important that we ourselves are healthy, both mentally and emotionally.

Home Climate

They used to say, and many still say it, "The hand that rocks the cradle rules the world." There is much truth in that as having to do with mental health, because the emotional environment determines so much of what personality, what outlook, what attitudes the child carries with him into adulthood. I refer to the climate of the home.

By climate I mean this: We look outside in the morning and we say that the weather is cold, warm, rainy, or whatever. We adjust accordingly, wearing appropriate clothing. And so in the home there is an emotional atmosphere that affects the way we behave.

Emotional Needs

In coming to specifics, every child has certain emotional needs. We are much concerned that he receives good food, plenty of sleep, exercise, and fresh air to grow healthy and strong. His emotional needs must be met equally as well if he is to be both healthy and happy.

Your child needs *love*, needs to feel that you — his

parents — love, want, and enjoy him. He needs to know that he matters very much to someone. The oft-repeated reason for so much crime and delinquency is "nobody cares for me." Your child needs to know that you do care what happens to him.

Your child needs *acceptance*, needs to believe that you like him just for himself, just the way he is — that you *always* accept him, even though you may not always approve of the things he does. He needs to develop his own particular personality and talents, and not be disowned because he doesn't fit into your dreams.

Your child needs *security*, needs to know that his home is a safe place, a shelter in time of crisis. It should be a place he can feel sure about, where both parents are on hand when he needs them most. He needs to know that he belongs to a family or group. To know there is a place where he fits in, where he's loved and wanted, gives any child security and peace of mind.

Your child needs *protection*, needs to feel that you will keep him safe from harm. When new and difficult and frightening situations arise he needs your help. For some situations you can prepare him in advance, giving him time to think through the experiences, showing how he should act. In these and in the unexpected experiences your nearness and your reassuring words and acts make him feel safe.

Your child needs some *independence*, needs to know that you want him to grow up. You should encourage him to try new things, to develop in his own way, barring that which would be harmful to him or to others. Your confidence in his ability to do things for himself when he is old enough helps develop satisfaction and appreciation.

Your child needs *control*, needs to know there are

limits to what he is permitted to do. He respects parents who inform him of these limits and hold him to them. He needs parents who will help analyze and direct his feelings of jealousy or anger, but who will not allow him to hurt himself or others when he has these feelings.

Your child needs *faith*, needs to have a set of moral standards to live by. He needs to believe in and respect human life and values — kindness, courage, honesty, generosity, justice, and purity. And with this set of human values he needs to know about the Author — God. All goodness, all "right living," has its basis in the eternal God and His laws and ideas. Through Him the child not only receives a pattern for living but also the power for living.

And how do you best satisfy such needs? Dr. Laban Peachey answers, "By being." It's not *telling* as much as it is *being* examples of mentally healthy people.

It's difficult to arrive at who or what is normal. Yet we somehow know and can tell who are the happy people who are able to solve the everyday problems of life. We also call it maturity.

Causes of Emotional Problems

Let's think about some causes of emotional problems. Our American culture is very complex. We live in an age of advanced education, of specialized training, of science and technology. Our daily lives bring many pressures to bear on us.

Our living in a state of movement and mobility is tearing out the roots of family and community ties. Such insecurity, instability, and aloneness in new and strange communities work against good mental health.

We can't remove all the causes. In fact, two people may live in the same environment; one may be healthy, able to take these things in stride; the other one cannot. It means having resources within ourselves to live above them.

Here is where faith plays a big part. Faith in God as the Author of right living helps anyone over problems and hurdles of our complex living. A belief in His love, in His concern, and in His power gives fortitude to meet each new and difficult experience. Faith to believe His forgiving power removes guilt and inner conflicts. It brings peace of mind beyond all human understanding or reasoning.

Proper Attitudes

I'd like now to suggest that a homemaker with a proper set of attitudes can eliminate much emotional tenrion. Let me illustrate.

What is your attitude toward being a housewife? Do you consider yourself important? You should. Home is the center of the universe and here characters are molded for life.

With such an attitude of your importance you can eliminate early-morning tension by getting up earlier. Dress neatly. Comb your hair as you did when first married. You'll feel better, and early rising will eliminate the rush.

Let's think about a rainy-day scene. The children are "whooping it up." Do you blame the rain? Do you panic and tell them, "I just don't know how to handle you kids!" Or do you introduce creative activities and help them become interested in their play?

This is a part of home climate which I mentioned as being important.

As parents, you should meet your child's emotional needs of love, acceptance, security, protection, independence, faith, guidance, and control. A healthy, happy child will become a mentally healthy adult — a good mate, a good parent, a good neighbor, a good worker, a good citizen.

The home atmosphere is as directly related to your family's health as is nourishing food, proper exercise, sufficient sleep, and rest. Your happy, cheerful, unworried approach to family life and love creates for them a relaxed, happy atmosphere. "Children in a home where there is love and where everyone has lots of fun, develop healthy attitudes toward health. They learn unconsciously to love life."[1]

Mother's Health

As you learn to relax you will be healthier and happier. Maybe you should become interested in a hobby that you enjoy which is absorbing and challenging. Yes, a hobby instead of another job, to "get away from it all." Do something outside of routine living — anything from gardening, to collecting gadgets, to the more strenuous joys of hunting, fishing, or hiking.

I'm a firm believer that faith, trust, and prayer to God help maintain a healthy body.

Nervous tension, worry, fear, and anger definitely produce illnesses, diseases, and emotional problems. As you know Jesus Christ and allow Him to bring peace, love, joy, and self-control to your thoughts and acts, these tensions and fears are gone. To the extent which you believe His promises, you become relaxed and calm. He even gives wisdom and a desire to observe necessary health rules. For your body belongs to Him.

Because your mental outlook on life is in harmony with the Creator of life, you will create an atmosphere conducive to good mental health for all the family.

8

Womanpower

One home-loving and contented mother of four small children became disturbed. She looked about her and noticed that most of her neighbors worked away from home because they wanted to. She began asking herself, "Who is right — are they, or am I? Where are mothers needed? Are they needed at home, or is it better to be out earning money?"

Many mothers feel guilty when they devote all their time, their love, and their energy to their families. Isn't that pathetic?

Those Who Must Work

Naturally there are those in any age or society who have no choice — wives of invalid husbands, widows, divorcees, or those who for some other reason have to become the family breadwinner.

Now to those who *must* work to keep the wolf away from the door, here are bits of advice gleaned from ones who have had to work. You must be aware that your job takes all your skill, your energy, and your patience. You'll be tired when you come home to do the housework, so watch your temper. Keep sweet. If you are married discuss the work with your husband. Share the needs and together work out ways to meet them. He'll sense that he belongs and is a part of the team. Also, include the children in this team work. This helps them develop a sense of security from the feeling that you take them into your confidence, that they too are needed and can contribute towards maintaining a decent home life.

Woman Power

I'd like to share with you some sobering statistics, sobering when we realize the impact of a mother's influence on her family for eternity. Sobering when we realize that many broken marriages and homes indirectly (if not directly) are a result of the change of the modern woman's interests.

Here are some of today's trend: "The divorce rate doubled since 1965, two-thirds of all mothers are in the working force — roughly double the rate in 1953, and more than half of all mothers of infants are in the work force." They break this down further into these facts: "In 1987, 37 percent of mothers working had children under six . . . 51 percent with children under one year of age."[1]

Several factors are involved such as the fact that modern laborsaving devices, semi-prepared foods, or even ready-cooked meals are easily available. But experts say the most important factor is that a job is a source of extra money and a means of satisfying the hunger for the luxuries of life, rather than from necessity or to "satisfy a driving ambition."

Our Standard of Living

Today's economy has subtly drawn mothers out of the home. They want the *things* money can buy. And it's so much easier to get meshed in with the tangible rather than the intangible, isn't it? The rewards, present and future, of dedicated mothering are intangible. And most of us haven't taken time out to think intelligently on the difference. The vacuum of swiftly moving materialism and accomplishments has sucked us into its gripping clutches. We're still whirling around unable to think straight.

A mother of three insists that if she doesn't work they couldn't have a "decent house with a safe place for her youngsters to play." But again her standard of decency may be a salary higher than someone else's.

One mother thought she *had* to work. It was impossible to save more than she did, yet when she worked, she became dissatisfied at the actual per hour income she brought home. After rethinking it through she found out that she *could* cut enough corners and stay home.

One working mother and her husband did some cold calculating. To their astonishment, they discovered that dollarwise they were not ahead, although she was earning a good salary. They figured transportation costs, extra clothes to appear in public, extra food costs, ready-made clothes for children, household help, and extra income tax. They totaled all this to find that about the only gain was tension, frustration, and a growing apart as husband and wife, and as a family.

The Love of Money

Again, I repeat that the lure of things, covetousness (wanting what others have), can very subtly draw us into its binding grip.

I think the Bible has a point to present right here. It doesn't say "Money is the root of all evil," but the "*love* of money." We should be sure that we are not victims of loving money to the extent that we neglect the true values of motherhood.

Educated Women

Not only our economic standard but also the education of women on a par with men has influenced mothers to work away from home. Education of women is fine, but why not also teach them how to use their knowledge and skill in the home setting? The tragedy is that it is assumed today that unless a woman takes her place beside men in the office, the laboratory, and the classroom, she is not using her education properly.

Anyone, even those with no preparation, can take up the "invaluable task of protecting young bodies, nurturing young minds, and indeed, creating the whole world of a young child," says popular opinion.

"Anyone can mop floors, wipe children's noses, change diapers, and open tin cans," it is argued. "The well-educated woman should leave these tasks to others and make a more valuable contribution to society through a worthwhile career." This is true, if the physical care is all that's involved in rearing children. But a child's general thought patterns and his basic behavior patterns aren't formed during mother's "off hours." They are a sum total of minute after minute, day after day, week after week, in association with others.

The educated mother can better answer the hundreds of daily questions. She can interpret life more intelligently. She can better follow the child in his school and community activities. She can use her knowledge of science, mathematics and her artistic and nursing skills within the framework of home. Education can help produce better wives and mothers if used in the proper way.

A Woman's Role as Wife

Let's just take a quick glance into a mother's role. First as wife, she is to be her husband's helper: spiritually, socially, mentally, and physically. They are to "become one" in their values and goals. But tell me, how is this possible when each goes his own way all day long? A tired, overworked, tense wife isn't much of a companion. And it's not a husband's role to come home and equally share the housework. I admire American men; they'll do it. They had to rise to the occasion. But the fact that he is apportioned his daily share of housework has driven more than one husband out of his home. It's one thing to offer to help, quite another thing to be assigned an equal share of the daily routine jobs.

The working wife overdevelops her masculine side, according to Florida Scott-Maxwell, a Scottish psychoanalyst. She loses her femininity. She overemphasizes her intellect and willpower which tends to diminish her tenderness, gentleness, understanding, and feeling ability. God created woman with the potential to develop sensitivity, compassion, kindness, "softness," and to have deep feelings with the depth of life. The working educated woman largely loses this, and no one presents the feminine feeling side of life to her husband and family. It's lost to the home and to society.

A Mother's Role

Mother is best endowed to love and train and teach her children. Her continual love, expressed so often in kisses and caresses, her closeness, her moment-by-moment concern, and her availability at all times, develop security in the child. As she goes about her daily household duties the children are there. They work together. They play together. They learn the deep lessons of life through informal daily living. She is the natural teacher of God and His truths. She shows Him to her children as she talks of Him, and she points Him out in nature and circumstances. " 'Mother' is the name of God in the lips and hearts of little children."

The Child Deprived of Love

A child psychiatrist says that young children, especially children under three, need some *one* person whom they know and trust to mother them. It could be an aunt or grandmother. But today's homes have eliminated them. It should be mother. You really can't count on anyone else.

Such statements should cause each one of us mothers to stop and think seriously. We know that today's children are more nervous, more insecure than was the past generation. How can it be otherwise if they're deprived of their basic need — moment-by-moment mother love? God knew why He established the home.

I sincerely believe He intended that the child would be tenderly nourished through a mother's love and tender care in those early impressionable years. She would be the major contributor to his or her early development.

Surveys taken among college students indicate that the high priority for them is to have a satisfying, happy marriage and home.

American adults regard a happy family life and a clean environment as indispensable. They want close friends and a successful career; a satisfying sex life is moderately important to them. Least important is a good income. Here are the result of a nationwide survey asking which of these things were essential or very important:

> Happy Family Life — 97%
> Clean Environment — 95%
> Close Friends — 85%
> Successful Career — 80%
> Satisfying Sex Life — 71%
> Good Income — 60%.[2]

Ask God to show you how you can contribute to making this desire for a happy home life possible for those in your home.

In conclusion, I ask, "Is womanpower channeled in the proper direction today?"

Remember, no amount of money or fame can satisfy like the love and trust of a husband and children.

9

Learn to Live

Recently I've really been "shook up," using today's terminology, as I have read about, heard about, and seen people who haven't learned how to live. People who don't know what a decent, happy life is. They are bored with life.

A popular magazine gave a five-and-one-half-page spread to the "greatest living playwright anywhere." The description of the seven plays he has written for Broadway is enough to make your hair stand on end. I won't describe the plots, but each one involves immorality. Murder, rape, alcoholism, and homosexuality are a few of the themes.

After this shock, the next day I opened a magazine to the page review of the shows of "the best company of modern dancers in the world," and read a description of one of the most popular television shows. Both of these reviews were saturated with sex and sordid living.

Then I turned the page and read that in just one city "south of the border" Americans spend one hundred twenty million dollars annually. Some of it goes to the over four hundred curio shops, but the larger part goes to the night clubs where sin and vice have no limits.

The next day a friend told me of a conversation she had overheard between several school teachers. Now these were respectable women in the community, mothers, and church attendants. One teacher asked if anyone knew where she could locate a certain book. The second teacher laughed, "Oh, you don't want that! It's a dirty book."

"Oh, yes I do," she retorted. "That's the kind I read. Whenever I hear the title of a dirty book or indecent movie that's what I read and see."

The third teacher added, "That's me. I get bored with the goody-goody stuff."

And the following morning as I glanced at a clipping handed to me by a friend, I was startled by these headlines: "The Housewife's Secret Sickness." Guess what it was . . . *alcoholism*. Probably one million American women are victims. The amazing thing to me, according to this article, is that they come from lovely homes with lovely families. Many are college graduates. Others are wives of professional men.

Why does a woman take to drink? She's bored with life and is trying to satisfy a void in her life with a bottle. She "has lost her way in life, and drinking has become a way of living."

Results

I feel sorry for these people I've mentioned, groveling in the low levels of self-centeredness, passion, and vice. They are bored with life and leisure. They think that to be a success means tangible results — a high bowling score, the latest model gadget, a blue-ribbon dog, or to belong to every club. They aren't really living. They aren't happy. They live through one day, hoping to think up something that will satisfy in the next, but they never find it. Second, I tremble at what such a low level of living will eventually do to our beloved land.

Primarily, God created women (and men) to glorify Him. And once a culture or a nation ignores this truth, it has no reason to exist. This has been proven over and over again in the Bible and in the history of past civilizations. God completely destroyed entire nations that lived such self-indulgent lives that He just couldn't stand them any longer.

I think it's high time that we wake up and learn to live. Yes, live according to the plan and purpose God set up for us. In order to do this we must know what life truly is. Then we must discipline ourselves in order to live such a life.

Secret of Real Life

This brings me to this truth. The secret of learning to live isn't in books and it isn't in a thought pattern. The secret of how to live is in identifying oneself with a person — that person is Jesus Christ.

True, living in union with Him does affect the books we read and enjoy. It does change our thought patterns. "In him was life; and the life was the light of men" (John 1:4).

God created man with the ability to fellowship with Him. But man sinned and became separated from God. Man was out of harmony with God's thoughts, His purposes, His ideals, and His goals for man. The Bible says that man is dead while he lives. And only as he comes back into harmony with God does he really live, live the full abundant life. And God gives us a true value of time. Too many of us are overawed with trinkets — houses, automobiles, furs

— but think little of the wealth of time.

God doesn't control us as the driver does his car. We must use our capacities. God works through them as we help ourselves.

Christ Changed Kate

Kate had been married ten years, but was bored most of the time. She felt walled-in and longed for the freedom of earlier years. She resorted to self-pity. She lacked nothing, bought extravagantly, and participated in every activity and entertainment, but was not happy. Her husband was losing his skill at work. She nagged him continually. One day she heard a speaker tell of the difference it makes when Christ takes over in a person's life.

Finally, at the end of herself and honestly wanting help, she opened up her heart to Christ. He cleansed her of all her guilt. She began reading the Bible and learned how He expected her to live. She learned that the greatest values of life are the intangible things, such as peace, love, and worthy goals. Her mind was completely changed. Her self-centeredness disappeared as she kept her gaze focused on Christ and His love for her. She began loving others and helping her neighbors and friends. She found joy in supporting her church program. Instead of criticizing and nagging she began expressing gratefulness for her husband's good qualities. She created a pleasant home for him and became his true companion. As she lost her life for him and others, to her amazement she found life. In several months her husband was promoted to the job he nearly lost. Just a coincidence? No indeed!

Kate learned to live through the transforming power of Christ. But she didn't sit in her easy chair and do nothing about it. God gave her the ideas and motivation to help herself.

I'd like to suggest some specific ways in which you can live life to its fullest, and make life worthwhile.

1. **Allow Christ to live in your heart.** Then keep His temple, your body, a fit place for Him to live. To be able to think right depends upon a clear brain. A clear brain depends on good blood. Good blood depends upon nourishing food, deep breathing, and proper exercise.

2. **Next, think deep thoughts.** Connect with the mind of God, whose thoughts are higher than our human ones. "Capture every thought until it acknowledges the authority of Christ" (2 Cor. 10:5;Phillips). In other words, your every thought must correspond with the ideals and truths of Christ. Think pure thoughts. Think honest thoughts. Think lovely thoughts. Think about the good in others. Keep your ideal, Christ, ever before you.

3. **Read good literature.** Read the bible daily. It contains truth. Learn to love great books and feed on masterpieces of literature. Memorize great passages, poems, and hymns. And, of course, memorize Scripture passages and verses. Use these to crowd out the negative and impure thoughts Satan will bring to your mind from time to time.

4. **Get interests outside of yourself.** When once you become truly interested in the good of each family member you'll have little time to think about your personal ego or gripes. As Kate found out, when you become absorbed in making others contented and happy, you find happiness and real living. Happiness never comes in searching madly for it, nor in self-indulgent living. It is a by-product as

you give yourself for others.

5. **Fellowship with those who can stimulate and help you,** those with whom you can share and discuss your goals and ideas. Unite with your local church family, and cooperate in its program to reach others with the gospel of Christ.

6. **Keep in close touch with Christ through daily prayer periods.** Commune with Him as you go about your work. Let Him give direction in your problems and decisions, and power to do what you know is right. And when on the spur of the moment you do wrong, right then and there confess it to God. Ask His forgiveness and believe that the blood of Jesus Christ cleanses you from all sin. Clean up immediately. It's a known fact that sin and guilt do cause many nervous disorders and sickness. The Bible says that the one who hides iniquity in his heart will not prosper. On the positive side, "No good thing will he [God] withhold from them that walk uprightly" (Ps. 81:11).

I'm sure that none of the millions of bored housewives want to be such. I'm sure that in their better moments, the millions who frequent shoddy entertainments long for a different kind of life. They long to face life's problems successfully, not to escape from them. They want to master wealth and leisure, to use them for God's glory and to help others, and not to be their victims. Only Jesus Christ can enable them to live abundantly. Only He can help one to really live. Jesus said, "I am come that they might have life, and that they might have it more abundantly" (John 10:10).

Remember, time is precious. It may soon run out. Live as though this were your last day. Learn to live Christ's way.

10

Accept Your Mother-in-Law

Ann fingered her purse and answered the counselor, "I couldn't take any more! No, we didn't live with Joe's parents, only one block from them. And every day, mind you, every day his mother called me up — asked about Joe and what I was doing. And now since the baby is here, she not only calls every day, but usually trots over once a day!" Ann paused.

The counselor questioned, "So your mother-in-law managed your lives?"

"No, not exactly," sighed Ann. "She occasionally gave advice, but not like some mothers-in-law I know. No, it wasn't that, but it's just her snooping into everything we did. Why can't she leave us alone? We aren't teenagers!"

Ann is typical of many young wives of today. This rebellion against in-law concern, and sometimes interference, is a part of our cultural change. Generations ago, in-laws often lived in the same house, partitioned to accommodate both families, or they lived in the "granddaddy house" in the same yard.

Dr. David R. Mace says that the core of the problem is generally the conflict between the two women — they are products of different generations, brought together by their love and interest in the same man. However, having said this, statistics show that at least one-fourth of all married couples have no in-law problems. I'm glad that many mothers-in-law are accepted and appreciated!

Avoid In-Law Tensions

Someone has this suggestion for avoiding in-law tensions: The young couple lays the foundations during courtship and engagement. They are not only marrying each other, they are marrying into each other's families. It's worth *any* effort to make themselves pleasing to each other.

Often in-law troubles are based on prejudices and resentments developed even before marriage. Of course, much could be said at this point about the parents, their acceptance of the daughter- or son-in-law. They should be courteous and kind, also. Even though Jack or Sue isn't the one they had picked out, they should avoid a critical attitude. Hostility doesn't help matters.

I think that planning the wedding together fosters good relationships. The young couple can afford to make a few concessions to insure future happiness in in-law relationships.

I observed this happening recently at my granddaughter's wedding. Both sets of parents were involved in the planning. I was greatly impressed when during the ceremony the officiating minister turned to the groom's parents and asked, "Do you accept Renee into your family?" Turning to the bride's parents he asked the same question, "Do you accept Jonathan into your family?" They both responded "We do."

And after the wedding, in-laws shouldn't be neglected. One wife, after a year of marriage, said to me, "I simply refuse to go to Joe's home every other Sunday. We have our own life to live."

I questioned, "Does it spoil your plans for entertaining?"

"No," she replied. "We have no other plans. But we want to be by ourselves."

I felt she was being selfish and very inconsiderate. Would it not have been better for them to accept the dinner invitation when nothing conflicted, and then excuse themselves early in the afternoon?

In our business and social life we learn to be considerate of others' wishes. We try to be courteous toward those we don't necessarily appreciate. Surely, if this can be done for purely commercial and social advantage, we can do as much for the sake of family peace.

Accept Her as a Person

The young wife should attempt to accept her mother-in-law as a person, as an individual. She should search for her good qualities and make friends with her. She should try to understand the adjusting it takes on the mother's part to suddenly "lose" a son, and not ridicule or criticize her to her husband.

The mother-in-law should be just as understanding. I like what one mother-in-law said: "I thought we'd lost a son, but it's worked out so differently — we've gained a daughter."

What I've mentioned concerning mother/ daughter-in-law relationships also holds for mother/

son-in-law relationships. The young husband should try to understand what it meant for her to give up a daughter. He should try to make friends with her. Treat her considerately.

Observing the Golden Rule and applying Christ's principle of losing self for others will help establish rewarding in-law relationships.

Try to Understand Her

Maybe the mother-in-law is critical and unhappy, but if the daughter-in-law would imagine how she feels, she would be more tolerant. "Kindness achieves so much and costs so little."

Dr. David R. Mace says that "most difficult mothers-in-law are really middle-aged women unadjusted to life. They are lonely, frustrated, craving attention . . . they need above all, warm affections and understanding. Yet, by their irrational, critical behavior, they cut themselves off more and more from the very thing they need."[1]

I think he makes a very significant statement: "unadjusted to life." All through life they probably have had a hard time getting along with anyone. And it could easily be a result of not having received love and security in their own home. What they do need is someone to show them how to love.

Lonely, a son gone — no longer sharing about the day's events or needing his clothes laundered; no longer asking for those good cookies "that only you can make, Mom."

Lonely, a daughter gone — who was always affectionate, who brought laughter and fun into the home and was a constant joy. Yes, a loneliness which they may not be able to analyze completely.

Maybe your mother-in-law is overcritical, or

imposes herself too much — at least you think so. Talk it over, try to appreciate her suggestions, even though you may not always incorporate them. And if you take time to sit down and plan some things together, this will make her feel she is wanted and appreciated.

Found the Answer

A wife who had very unhappy relationships with her mother-in-law, to the extent that they produced migraine headaches, finally found the answer as far as her part was concerned:

1. Be filled with the love of Christ and sincerely love that mother- and father-in-law the way Christ loves them. It is human nature to tend to rebel or retaliate with unkind and critical remarks, but the love of Christ constrains (controls) us.

2. Do all the kind and thoughtful things for them you can think of. It may be a small thing like remembering their birthdays or anniversary.

3. Don't tell a lot of persons your problems, but do not keep it to yourself. Find one person to tell, in whom you can confide and find help.

4. Last, but not least, do not harbor any feelings of self-pity. Remember, it is a sin. It will damage your character and affect your moods so greatly that even your children will detect them. Christ made me recall all the cruelty, shame, and reproach He had to bear without even one unkind word being said. Remember, if you accept your mother-in-law as a friend, if you try to understand her and show her the same thoughtful gestures and loving courtesies you would another, you will have happy, rewarding relationships with her.

Mother, If You Wouldn't Mind

Why should I call you mother-in-law
You who have been so kind?
I'd really rather just call you mother,
That is, if you wouldn't mind.

For I feel so like a daughter to you
And I need your love so much,
So why should I call you mother-in-law
When it doesn't seem like you're such?

From the very first time I saw your smile
I knew somehow inside
That your love was deep as the deepest sea
And Oh, just twice as wide.

I might have known it all along —
How could the man who's now mine
Be so perfect, so grand in ev'ry way
Without a mother so fine?

But I have something other than this
To call you mother for
I'm sure that this would be reason enough
But Oh, there's much more.

You took me into your heart, your life,
You taught me many things
Life faith in God and in others, too,
Like love and its hidden springs.

Oh, why should I call you mother-in-law
When you're everything nice combined?
I'd rather just call you mother, please,
That is, if you wouldn't mind.[2]

11

The Whip of Hurry

Hurry! Hurry! Hurry! Where to? Why? Is it worth it?

Gone are the days of relaxed hours on the porch swing, visiting the neighbors, piecing quilts, crocheting, or knitting leisurely.

Several weeks ago, while driving through a modest residential district, I noticed several ladies sitting on a porch enjoying the lovely day and each other. I thought to myself, *How rare! But how peaceful and serene!*

A Daily Rush

Too many days are scheduled to the minute. Then, when the unexpected turns up we are frustrated! It's nearly impossible to fit it into our schedule. If we do, then something else is shoved aside until *manana* (tomorrow). But when morning comes there are other tasks vying for immediate attention. Someone has called this a mad rat race.

A native chief, treasurer of an administration in Nigeria, broadcast his impressions of England during a brief visit: "Everything and anything was in swift motion. Vehicles in their thousands, right and left, thousands of men, women and children running about as if certain elements were changing them. This atmosphere made me conclude that the country itself was in motion. Unless you move fast you are either knocked down by a vehicle or by the pedestrians. No one can afford to lose a minute."[1]

This description sounds much like our country, doesn't it? Men drive dangerously fast, only to arrive at their destination to do nothing worthwhile. Often women rush furiously to finish the necessary household tasks and then spend hours reading a romantic novel or engaging in some other entertainment that never benefits them one bit! It neither makes them more helpful wives nor more loving mothers, but slyly leads them into fantastic, unrealistic experiences that make them dissatisfied with reality.

"Once a man would spend two weeks waiting if he missed a stage coach. Today he raves if he misses the first section of a revolving door."[2]

Is It Profitable?

A friend passed this saying on to me: "The hurrier I am, the behinder I get!" How true! Just another way of saying, "Haste makes waste," isn't it?

Hurry leads to mental and physical breakdown. It hinders us in seeing those intangible, important values of life.

I read of a successful business executive who was on the verge of a nervous breakdown. One day a clergyman friend of his entered his office. The businessman expressed his frustrations and asked for advice. Without reply the friend lifted his motto from the desk and dropped it into the wastebasket. The motto read, "Do It Now!"

I'd be the last one to suggest procrastination for a mother in the home. But I'm fully aware that with the dozens of pressures of today's society — community, school, church, besides our family — we can't do everything, even with hurrying. And we don't want to be shirkers. We want to do all we can to help others. Yet, I believe we often forget that "in quietness and in confidence ... [is our] strength," not in hurrying to and fro and neglecting the important values.

We Hurry the Toddler

Not only do we adults cringe under this whip of hurry that's held over our backs, but we're holding the same over our children's lives.

"Now hurry, baby, finish your food." Then we wonder why his stomach is upset! "Hurry up, what's the matter with you?" There's no time for walks or enjoying life about us.

Mother decides to visit a friend or go to the park. In a hurry she dresses the toddler, puts him in the stroller, and away they go. She arrives more quickly, to be sure, but toddlers like to get close to things. They like to examine a stone, a leaf, a flower, the hedge. Being restrained in a stroller on such occasions keeps the child from the fun of learning what's smooth and what's prickly. Relaxed walks with mother are valuable learning experiences for the child. Mother can point out the beauties and wonders of nature. Or call attention to interesting landmarks, houses, trees, birds, and animals, and in this way teach the child to be observant.

A "Rush" School Morning

This "hurry, hurry" doesn't stop with the toddler or preschool-age child. When he is getting ready to go to school, for too many the morning is a time of rush, tension, and scolding. This is easily remedied if mother disciplines herself to get up early enough to allow sufficient time for everyone to prepare for the day unhurriedly. And small children need more time to dress, eat, and to find their books than we parents do. Why wait until the last minute before calling the child? Wouldn't it be conducive toward a happier morning if he would get up in ample time and help a bit with household routine? At least get himself ready?

Dr. Leslie J. Mason, Professor of Education, University of Southern California, says that the morning rush isn't "just for an hour." It sets the tenor for your child's whole day. And I'd like to add, for us parents, too! The child who leaves home with parental shouts still ringing in his ears isn't ready for the challenge of the day.

A tense child is uncooperative and unfriendly. He can't apply himself to work, or even to play. The teacher is unable to cope with the situation. His day has been ruined because he's been wrongly disciplined with the whip of hurry at the beginning of the day.

The Whip of Hurry Continues

This continues with the older child: "Hurry, it's time for your club meeting." "Hurry, let's get this job done. In half an hour it must be finished." And so one day follows the other.

We hurry their eduction with extra loads and

summer school. Quick, so they'll be prepared for a career while young. More years to make more money!

Many parents, especially mothers, are guilty of hurrying their sons and daughters into social activities years before they are ready emotionally. Mother worries because daughter has no dates at twelve years of age. She pushes this twelve-year-old child into wearing makeup, and dressing and acting like a young woman. Now I know this isn't true of all mothers, but I was shocked to read that in some areas mothers do arrange dates, dancing parties, and other social activities for their twelve-year-olds. They want them to become social butterflies.

I recall several years ago, in one community some parents felt resentful because their children weren't included in all the extracurricular activities at school. One parent who heard this was shocked, because at their house they were battling with the problem of trying to teach their boys that they didn't need to participate in every activity. Home and family projects are important, too!

Rushed Away from Home

Nowadays youngsters hurry to the marriage altar. On this score, we no doubt try to slow them down, but if they've been raised to the tune of hurry since birth, why slow down here?

We've hurried them away from home. Now we have years to regret — years in which to wish we would have taken time to live, to enjoy life to its fullest.

Several years ago a mother said to me,

Oh, how I wish I could begin again!
How differently I would raise my children!
We were always in a rush. I had to have my

house in perfect order. I belonged to many outside organizations. When at home it was rush, rush, rush, all day long. I never took time to enjoy their hobbies, or nature around us, or to enter into their world! It was hurry to meet my schedules!

I felt sorry for this mother. Her children were scattered across the country. They seemed disinterested in their parents' problems and activities, as well as in their religion.

The Bible Says

The Bible says that the person who is in a hurry with his feet sins: "He that hasteth with his feet sinneth" (Prov. 19:2). The person with a hasty spirit magnifies folly: "He that is hasty of spirit exalteth folly" (Prov. 14:29).

Furthermore, it says that the thoughts of those in a hurry tend toward want. There's much lacking in the thoughts of the hurried mind. Not only does this hurry-hurry spirit drive us through the day, but it affects our thought life. It leaves no time for meditation, relaxation, and recreating of mind, soul, and body. It affects our speech and our decisions. We fail to take time to wait on God for Him to work, or even to give Him a chance to tell us what to do.

Let's take time to analyze the cause of our hurry. Let's carefully discuss its effect upon us and our families. Then with God's help let's slow up, ease our load, and cut off tension.

Don't discipline your children with the whip of hurry. In the relaxed, quiet mind there is great strength.

12

Limit Your Activities

Mary happily accepts her new role as home-maker. It challenges her! She loves her family. She willingly and happily gave up a full-time job when the first baby came. She had no problem in this decision. But Mary is caught in something that could be disastrous.

Her telephone keeps ringing. The president of the hospital auxiliary, Boy Scouts, PTA, the women's missionary group, and the heart fund call begging her to participate. They need her so badly! No one will take the job!

She finds herself flitting from one good organization to another. Her evenings are full. Spare moments are spent in preparation and planning rather than in relaxed times with her family.

Too Many Activities
Vance Havner says in his book *Pleasant Paths,*[1] "I am convinced that if the Devil can't make us lazy, he'll make us so busy here and there that the best is

sacrificed for the good."

This is so true! The Devil knows that a wife holds the key to her husband's happiness. He knows that a mother shapes the lives of the children. If he can get her so busy doing good things that she's frustrated, tired, and irritable when at home, unable to develop warm relationships with the family, then he has won a major victory, for the home is the basic unit of society, of the church, of the community, and of the nation.

A "Heart to Heart" listener wrote, "I do believe our biggest problem is too many meetings . . . . It's a way to escape responsibilities. In my neighborhood, most mothers are attending meetings or on the go somewhere, while their children run the road."

Good Activities
Another young "Heart to Heart" listener has questions on this very pertinent problem:

> How do you curb some church activities, when the church program is crammed full, night after night the year round. Each one is good . . . but our pastor and some members associate the depth of a person's spirituality by the faithfulness in attendance and participation in *every* activity.
>
> The faithful few who appear for everything are praised and the others scolded. How do we escape this stigma?

You Must Decide
This homemaker presents today's dilemma. These are all good, worthwhile activities and organizations, "But where do I belong? How can I refuse and keep

from feeling guilty?" These feelings haunt many.

There's no pat answer. Each homemaker must decide for herself, but she must always be conscious that her primary ministry is in the home.

Home is your most important duty. It's your highest calling. This calls for **you** to be on the job, to be available.

You must also take a long-range view. Your children will be on their own before very many years. Then with much free time you can join those activities of your choice. In those earlier years you can keep informed. You may be able to give limited time. Someone has said that it is better to serve **one** cause well than to spread your energies thinly over many activities.

To decide what to accept or what to reject is not a one-time decision. It requires continued thought and decisions.

I hope, if presently you can participate in only one outside activity, that you will choose a prayer fellowship. This, to me, is the most rewarding and fruitful outside activity a busy homemaker has.

I believe with all my heart that we women have this special calling. Obviously, we cannot belong to every worthwhile organization. We may be confined at home. Yet through prayer we can travel into many lands, into many institutions, into many organizations, locally or far away. Even if you cannot leave home you can go on wings of prayer.

Avoid Conflicts

But even church activities may conflict with family needs. So you must keep this in mind.

I recall years ago I was preparing a topic for the World Day of Prayer meeting. There were many interruptions. I became very upset. And then I read the verse I was incorporating in the talk: "If we live in the Spirit, then let us also walk in the Spirit."

I was "living" in my thought with God, but I wasn't walking "in the Spirit," wasn't taking one step at a time with Him. Probably, I should have canceled that engagement because of the pressures it placed on me at that time, and taken the few moments I had daily for the children.

That hasn't been the last time either! I believe this problem of outside activities hits me harder than anyone else! I've searched long for an answer.

Identify with Husband

Now I want to think of family needs and the tragic consequences when you neglect your family. You need to understand your husband and identify with him. This requires daily time, thought, and energy.

One young wife bitterly sobbed her story to the marriage counselor. Bill had begun to treat her indifferently. He no longer showed interest at home. But as she refreshed her memory, she recalled that it started the year she became chairman of the weekly youth group. The night of their meeting conflicted with her husband's only night at home.

I'm reminded of a letter from a young homemaker. She wrote,

> We, too, have the problem of getting too busy. It's hard to know, especially when engaged in the Lord's work, just when to say "no." A remark my doctor made to me once has stuck in my mind and has often helped my dear husband and me . . . I made some statement saying we didn't have very

much time together because we were so busy in the Lord's work.

He replied, "Your being together is the Lord's work!" This impressed me coming from the lips of a non-Christian.

If a wife is too busy, even in church work, to have some relaxed, unhurried time alone with her husband, she will soon lose him.

Understand Children

A mother needs to understand and identify with each child, as well as with her husband. Seventeen-year-old Sally opened up her lonely heart to her counselor. "My mother's civic and church activities keep her so busy that she hasn't time for her own family. That's why her love lacks understanding and identification."

If mother is too busy, even in good service, to pay loving attention to the important world of her daughter or son, she will lose them, and they will be too busy to have time for God.

Mothers don't have a monopoly on this problem of outside activity. The whole family gets caught in this gale. Parents should direct and provide time for pleasant, meaningful relationships together as a family.

Time for God

Not only do too many outside activities rob us of time for loving and understanding each family member, they also rob us of time for God. That time of spiritual refreshment — the source of right attitudes, of true concern, of wise understanding, and Christ-like love. A time when we dump our cares and troubles on God and find peace and courage.

You and I know homemaking is important. We feel the terrific pull of good activities. But what can we do?

Just today the Lord let an article come to my attention, written by Charles Hummel, a busy Christian leader. He says he has to have time with God. A time when before God he schedules the day's jobs — listing them in order, giving priority to the tasks to be done. He must keep appointments at a minimum, to allow for this time of fellowship with God.

His solution to accepting too many outside calls is this: When a call comes over the telephone he asks time to pray about it. Regardless of how clear the calendar looks at the moment, he delays the answer for one or two days. If the event still seems important two days later, after he has counted the cost, then it is more likely to be God's will. I again quote Vance Havner: "We display the Lord's leading as much by what we refuse as by what we accept."[2] The Lord doesn't operate on a full-quota daily basis. He knows we often can do more by doing less. His concern is quality, not quantity.

The Solution

I think these men of God, Mr. Hummel and Mr. Havner, have something that will work for a homemaker. Two days' time for reflection, for discussing it with husband and family, for talking it over with God, and waiting His answer, before accepting any outside responsibility.

It this your answer?

I like this solution. It's the answer for me.

And, I believe, for any homemaker!

13

When Trouble Strikes

Every homemaker has her share of troubles because she and the family are human and subject to natural laws. The washer breaks. The baby cries several hours in the night. Johnny cuts his toe. There are misunderstandings.

But these soon pass. She does well not to keep thinking about them because "troubles, like babies, grow larger by nursing."

The homemaker shouldn't **make** trouble either by thinking of what might happen, because the shadow of a trouble is usually blacker than the trouble itself. "Of all our troubles, great or small, the greatest are those that don't happen at all."

There are also the times of deep sorrow, suffering, disappointment, and failure which seem insurmountable. These may drain our strength, silence our songs, open the wells of self-pity and complaint, and produce mental and physical illness, or they may be stepping-stones to a nobler life.

Troubles Are Windows

In a touching story, a young mother relates how trouble struck their home. The newly born babies, twin girls, completed their happiness — but only briefly, for soon she knew one of the babies had a harelip.

"Why did **this** happen to **us**? Why did **God** allow it?" she sobbed. Soon her anguish gave way to rational thought. She began reminding herself that there was much to be thankful for. It was corrective. Instead of doubting God, she remembered that "love dependent on what the eye sees is not love at all." They would love this baby. That was the first step. She **accepted** her trouble.

Next, she steeled herself to master the technique of feeding the baby with what looked like an oversized hypodermic syringe. That was her second step. **She did something constructive** about her problem.

When the twins were brought home, five-year-old Sue questioned, "Why did God make her lip like **that?**"

Her father replied that sometimes it looks as though God makes mistakes, and added, "But He gave her to us anyway, because He knew we would love her just the same."

Sue beamed, "He was right, wasn't He?" That was step number three. They **didn't doubt God.**

The baby developed as a normal child. Several operations were performed to correct the lip. Now she talks as clearly as her sister. One more operation is need for her appearance to be as normal as her twin's.

A disfigured, frightened baby has been transformed into a lovely, self-confident, happy child, with a normal life ahead of her, because her parents made a window out of their trouble and saw their daughter in the years to come.

You can use trouble as a mirror, seeing only yourself, your shattered hopes, your desires. Or you can use trouble as a window through which you see something greater than yourself, where you see something beautiful and majestic — something that will bless others for years to come.

Bunyan used a prison to produce the world's second best seller, *The Pilgrim's Progress*. Fanny Crosby used blindness to give Christendom some of the greatest hymns it has known.

Sorrow Is Fruit
Victor Hugo said, "Sorrow is fruit: God does not make it grow on limbs too weak to bear it."

I'm thinking just now of a former classmate of mine, a pastor's wife and mother of three boys. For many years she has lain helpless in an iron lung; nevertheless, from her room of pain and suffering have gone out many women, blessed with a new devotion and love for God and life. She has also blessed many through her poems.

Suffering Is a School
Many of life's lessons are learned in the school of suffering. "The school of suffering graduates rare scholars."

God often uses trouble to trim the sharp edges from our personalities in order to make us loving, kind, and sympathetic.

God has taught me many lessons from troubles. They also seem to be God's examination. It's like this: I discover a new promise, or a new truth about God. My entire heart responds. "I believe, Lord, it's true, because You've said so." Then soon comes a difficult situation in which I need to apply the very truth I've newly discovered. God wants to see if I've really learned the lesson.

A number of years ago the verse "In everything give thanks" was impressed upon my mind. I used it to keep content in the small, irritating events of an isolated life, often alone with four little children. But when suddenly God allowed a nervous breakdown and removed us from the mission field in Argentina, I'll admit I fumbled a bit in that examination! However, the master Teacher stayed close by. I soon was able to write the correct answer. Sometimes the learning process is difficult and slow.

Troubles Bring Blessings

When troubles come, remember God wants you to get to the end of yourself, to turn to Him in utter abandonment. In your nothingness, you don't hinder God's strength.

Through sickness you come to a standstill for a time of mediation and a time of prayer for you and for others. "Be still and know that I am God" is His command.

Troubles and difficulties acquaint you with an almighty, powerful, miracle-working God with whom anything is possible. They increase your faith. Through trouble God becomes real and personal.

The Lesson

I loved the sunshine warm and bright,
And walked with great delight;
But sometimes on those pleasant days
I wandered far from wisdom's ways.
And then the deep, dark shadows fell,
For my dear Lord, who loves me well,

Did know that in the darkness dim,
I'd seek for solace close to Him.
In time He bade the shadows go,
When I had fully learned to know
It matters not if skies be clear,
But only this — that He is near.
                    — Author Unknown

How Do You React?

When trouble strikes, do you protest, "If God is love, He wouldn't do **this to me**!"

Really, God doesn't *make* you suffer, but He does allow it to come.

God understands human nature perfectly. He knows that without suffering and difficulties we human beings would forget that we are created for His glory. We'd get self-sufficient, with no need of Him.

I recall the words of an aged blind man, minus arms, who read his Braille Bible with his tongue: "I thank God daily for the accident that took my sight and my arms. If this wouldn't have happened, I would have continued in my own selfish ambitions, then spent eternity in hell. God had to bring me low, so I'd look up — to Him."

Cause of Suffering

"Is suffering punishment from God?"

No, not at all. Some comes as a natural result of breaking natural laws. You go out in the chilly air, scantily dressed, and you'll doubtless catch a bad cold.

Some suffering comes from the powerful evil force, direct from Satan's kingdom. We may pay the penalty of sin in one way or another — in body, mind, emotions, or personality. Even forgiven sin may leave its mark. The mother who in anger cruelly beats an innocent child may care for a cripple the remainder of her life, even though God has forgiven.

Some people suffer from their own faults. The wife who nags at her husband from morning till night may suddenly find herself unloved or alone.

Some good people suffer from those who are condemned by a good life. The Bible tells us that the wicked Queen Herodias, who was living in adultery, ordered John the Baptist killed because his teaching condemned her.

However, we may suffer as chastisement or discipline from God. As a father disciplines the child whom he loves, so God disciplines us as His children.

We Find God

In time of trouble we are helpless. There's no one else to go to, so we turn to God. We grasp the ropes of faith swinging from His hands. Then gently He pulls us up from the pit of distress.

When trouble strikes, accept it. God has allowed it to come. Use it as a window through which you see something grand as a result. Do something constructive about your trouble. God promises you the grace you need. Just turn it over to Him to remove in His time, in His way. Or to give you victory and joy through it. Remind yourself often of His words: "Call upon me in the day of trouble: I will deliver thee, and thou shalt glorify me" (Ps. 50:15).

14

Why Be Lonely?

Some years ago a beautiful actress, supposedly with everything a young girl could want, took her life. A brief note explained why — she was unbearably lonely. Not that she was alone, not at all! She was continually surrounded by people, but lonely!

It has been said that people are lonely because they build walls instead of bridges.

Someone else has concluded that "loneliness is not so much a matter of isolation as of insulation."

It seems to me they are saying that loneliness, that awful despairing feeling, is not dependent on location, vocation, or even rejection, but on one's attitude toward it.

Lonely Dina

Dina was always a lonely girl. Her parents were divorced. They placed her in winter boarding schools and summer camps.

When on her own, at eighteen, she worked hard and visited her mother on weekends. But she had no friends.

When she saw families together a wave of loneliness enveloped her. One time she stood outside a public building, frequently looking at her watch, as though awaiting someone. Finally, she entered alone. It never occurred to her that she might join a church or YWCA group.

But finally she moved to a business girls' residence. The German cook, Inger, soon changed her life.

One afternoon only Dina and one other girl were in the house. They smelled gas and rushed downstairs to the kitchen. There lay Inger, dead. Inger's note revealed her loneliness, although she had been living among happy, carefree girls. They laughed and joked, but not with her. To Inger, America was hard and cold.

That night Dina thought long of the tragic event. Inger was lonely but she had not tried to find out the reasons she was unloved. She had retreated behind her self-made wall of silence. She could have opened the door. But she lacked the will. And her wall collapsed on her.

Dina Thinks of Others

Since that day Dina thinks of others. She goes out of her way to say hello to people she meets, to lend a helping hand to the neighbor next door or to the young mother nearby.

In the apartment house where she lives are fifty family units. They live so close, yet many are lonely. Some have never spoken to each other in the twenty years she has lived there.

On day Dina took her daughter to play in the park and sat down beside another mother, then asked how old the baby was.

The young mother burst out in tears. When asked what was wrong, she replied, "You're the only person who has spoken to me since I came two weeks ago."

Dina asked, "Have you spoken to someone?"

The young mother hadn't thought of that.

There are many lonely hearts because they make themselves lonely. No one pays any attention to them so they build walls around themselves when they could build bridges over which to travel to happiness and security.

> Art thou lonely, O my brother?
> Share thy time with another!
> Stretch a hand to one unfriended,
> And thy loneliness is ended.
> — John Oxenham

Solitude

There is the loneliness of solitude. This, however, is good for anyone. A child must have moments of aloneness. Not that he's rejected, but time to just think, dream, or read.

A young mother read a article on the treasures of loneliness which appeared in a popular magazine. Then in grateful response she wrote that it had helped them to decide to stay where they are. They loved the country charm of their home, but had begun to worry about their girls missing out on having many friends and all the technical advantages of city life. But she did feel that aloneness could force them to learn how to use their time beneficially. This mother concluded, "It's hard to fight the trend toward constant activity and little thought or study, but we are pulling hard for the few who are trying to use their brains instead of cars all the time."

Cause of Unsocial Conduct

A prominent psychologist says that loneliness is

the underlying cause of unsocial conduct. The child, alone in a family because mother and daddy didn't want him or don't love him, soon covers up his hurt and his hungry heart by being sulky, by withdrawing to himself, or by silence. Or he may be hostile and defiant. All he really wants is someone to understand and to love him.

Much of today's juvenile delinquency is attributed to loneliness. These youngsters need to belong to someone. Parents have not given themselves. Oh, they've given things and money and prestige, but no companionship. Children must belong, so they join a gang. They want recognition — and they soon get it.

> Alone with a book by a fire — that's well.
> Alone on the dunes — there's a certain spell
>   to that.
> Or alone is a pleasant way to go for a walk on
>   a stormy day.
> It's thrilling alone, with the reins in hand
> And to be alone, with some work is grand.
> Alone in a mist, with a moon — that's magic.
> Alone on a Saturday night — that's tragic.
>   — Margaret Engleman

Two Roads

Sven Stolpe points out in his biography of Dag Hammarskjöld[1] that this brilliant and gifted man, the former secretary general of the United Nations, was tormented constantly by loneliness.

However, he did something about it. Something constructive and creative. He looked realistically at his problems of loneliness and turned to the only One who could fill the lonely heart. He turned to God. Only after his death did many of his friends discover the depth of his spirituality.

Loneliness! A baby, a small child, an adolescent, a youth, an adult — each one needs to know he is accepted and belongs to someone, to something. Loneliness drives you to despair, to withdrawal, to utter defeat, as it did the lonely star who committed suicide.

Or it may drive you, as it did Dag Hammarskjöld, to dig down to its roots and conquer it. How? By finding a new source of power, a new identity through Jesus Christ, a new sense of belonging. Instead of thoughts and plans turning inward to self and self-pity, they focus beyond self to Him — the One who is "closer than breathing, and nearer than hands or feet." That's what loneliness did for me.

I Have Felt Loneliness

I have felt the deep loneliness of location
    — often separated from my family.
I have felt the weary loneliness of a hospital bed
    — with no one near to comfort.
I have felt the loneliness of aloneness —
    in a strange land, pressed on every side by
    many people.
I have felt the loneliness of wifehood —
    when my husband's tasks took him away,
    often and long.
I have felt the loneliness of tremendous
    temptation — when even God seemed far away.
I have felt the loneliness of misunderstanding —
    when justice mocked and laughed.
I have felt the loneliness of standing for the right
    — while others looked on in pity.
I have felt the loneliness of deeply involved
    decision — which no one else could solve.
I have felt the loneliness of a shadow of death —

when breath stood aloof.
At times I still experience loneliness.
But in every situation I focus on God, on His
    words in the Holy Scriptures.
I talk to Him. He lifts me above the despair of the
    moment to himself — and to others.
I forget aloneness — rejection — suffering —
    misunderstanding — sorrow.

— Ella May Miller

I remember how comforting the words of this chorus were:

How can I be lonely
When I've Jesus only
To be my companion
And unfailing guide?
How can I be weary
Or my life seem dreary
When He's walking
By my side!

— Haldor Lillenas

You, too, can belong to God — right now. He'll fill your loneliness with a presence, a companionship, a power, a joy, and a purpose you have never known before.

Why be lonely?

15

Can You Afford to Hate?

Hatred is self-punishment. It's a boomerang which will hit you harder than the person you throw it at.

Mrs. Paine, a cultured woman respected and admired by her friends, can't bear the sight of her neighbor Sally. Whenever the two women happen to meet, Mrs. Paine hurls a cutting remark. She takes a quick pass at Sally's clothes, her flowers, or something else. When they were young coeds, Sally won the coveted position as campus queen. Although an event of years past, Mrs. Paine continues to nurture the seed of hatred. Nourished and sheltered, it has never stopped growing. It occasionally bears fruit in the form of migraine headaches.

Mrs. Blank faithfully nurses her arthritic pains. No day passes without rehearsing to someone her ills, plus complaints about her daughter-in-law. Although she lives in a cozy apartment in her son's lovely home, her hostility gives way to complaints about extravagance, child care, and the younger woman's cooking.

Hate Poisons

In both cases hate, expressed in resentment, criticism, and revenge, caused physical ailments. Researchers have found many cases of rheumatic arthritis resulting from resentment. Unforgiveness, grudges, and unkind attitudes can work themselves up to violent anger. Hatred is poison throwing its venom into the mind and body, creating physical illnesses and disturbances, and causing many emotional diseases.

Dr. William C. Menninger, late president of Menninger Foundation, Topeka, Kansas, says, "The key to good mental health is the ability to handle hostile feelings."

The most unhappy life is one full of hatred, for hate poisons the heart. It makes life miserable.

Forgive and Forget

It isn't easy to forgive a wrong done against you. Especially a deliberate act done by one whom you had trusted and in whom you had confidence!

But as you forgive, you can forget. Then, and only then, can you suppress the thoughts of wrong, retaliation, and revenge. Only then can Christ's love enter your heart and mind.

Just before Leonardo da Vinci commenced work on his famous *Last Supper*, he had a violent quarrel with a fellow painter. The enraged and bitter Leonardo determined to take revenge by painting the face of his enemy, the other artist, into the face of Judas. But when he came to paint the face of Christ, he could make no progress. Something held him back, frustrating his best efforts. He came to the conclusion that it was because he had painted his enemy into the face of Judas. He erased the face of Judas and commenced anew on the face of Jesus, a success acclaimed through the ages.

"That is a profound parable of the Christian life. You cannot at one and the same time be painting another face with the colors of enmity and hatred."[1]

Hate Is Learned

"I simply hate him!" snarls Bee, in mentioning her husband. And she doesn't have to tell anyone. Her actions, looks, and words are a dead giveaway.

Their home is literally hell on earth!

Bee's children have long ago caught the spirit of hate, ill will, and revenge. And yet she complains about their actions, and questions why they can't be nice to each other!

Children learn to hate. It often begins within the family circle. The first time Jacky strikes angrily at his sister and says, "I hate you," is the time to nip that attitude in the bud. Later it will have become a customary thing.

Mother should say, "Jacky, there's no reason to get angry and talk like that. Go outside and run up and down until you've worked off your anger. Don't come in until you say to sister, 'I love you.' "

But how useless is such an approach if mother harbors hate. How useless if mother and father hate each other!

A family poor in material possessions but with love in their hearts, is richer than a millionaire family with hate in their hearts.

The Bible mentions this, and today's terminology would read "It is better to eat soup with someone you love than steak with someone you hate" (Prov. 15:17;LB).

Vaccinate against Hate

In the home children learn either to hate or to

love other races.

A father questioned his son concerning the commotion on the street, "What was your fun?"

"Oh," he answered casually, "we were just licking a Jew boy."

Father continued, "Why? What had he done?"

"Nothing . . . ."

In surprise the father took his son's hand and hurried down to find the mistreated boy. In vain they hunted. At last the father said, "We will try to find him tomorrow and then you can ask his pardon."

Later in the evening father and son looked at books with Jewish authors. He related stories of Jewish boys: Joseph, David, Daniel. He told of the Saviour, Christ. He acquainted the son with famous Jewish scientists.

That night as he lay asleep in his bed, the boy turned and tossed. Mother felt his forehead. "I believe he is a little feverish."

"That's not surprising," volunteered the father. "Today I vaccinated him against the meanest of all mean and vulgar diseases — hate."

Only as we parents learn to appreciate the good qualities of another will we help our children overcome hatred of race — any race. Otherwise, we are perpetuating a generation of hating people. "The tight skirts of hate and prejudice shorten the steps of progress."

A psychiatrist, David M. Levy, says, "If we knew as much about mental health as we do about physical health, an epidemic of hate would be considered as dangerous as an epidemic of typhoid."

The adult who as a child did not experience the sacrificial love of parents, or who has no one to love or to give him love, is the person who hates. Furthermore, he can't tolerate minority groups.

Upton Close says that,

> Hate is only right when we hate the evil, when we hate a better-than-thou attitude. To hate what causes war, to hate a way of life that denies others their place in the sun . . . to hate race and creed discrimination is the only hate that will win lasting peace.[2]

Love Replaces Hate

But how can I overcome hate?

God's heart of love answers: "Love your enemies . . . do good to those who mistreat you . . . return evil with good . . . pray for those you hate you" (Matt 5:44;free trans.).

"Easier said than done," you immediately reply.

Granted, but it's possible.

First, you must be aware of your need, and accept the fact that "God is love" and that He loves you. Ask His forgiveness. He deals harshly with sin but loves the sinner. And when you experience His mercy and His love, manifested through forgiveness of your wrongs, then you experience His acceptance of you — just as you are. Then, and **only then,** can you accept others and love them with His kind of love.

Second, you learn to love by loving. I once heard it said, "You learn to speak by speaking, to study by studying, to run by running; and just so you learn to love God and man by loving. Begin as an apprentice."

As parents we teach our children to love by demonstrating love to each other, to them, and to all peoples.

Instead of becoming skilled in hate, always on the lookout for finding evil in everyone and everything, try the opposite. Hunt for good. Beside the person's name or the race that you hate, write the quality you like the most. Read it several times daily. One man actually did this and soon his stomach ulcers were greatly improved. Read accounts of such worthwhile projects: The domestic peace corps pilot project in New York City's Harlem employs assistant teachers in remedial reading classes. Most of the fifty-eight teachers are Negroes. In other cities, agencies are introducing workshops and courses to aid skilled Negro workers and employers to locate each other. Maybe you can "swap" children for a week or two with a Negro family as some are doing in Rochester, New York, or with children of other ethnic groups.

Love Is the Key
Love is the key that opens hearts,
  That puts smiles onto faces,
That tears the masks of hate apart,
  That has no creed or races.
In the USA, or Timbuktu,
  It's welcomed, understood;
No other thing could ever do
  The miracles love could.
When he loves God, the artist paints,
  The poet writes his songs,
The goodly bow and become saints,
  The sinner turns from wrongs,
A stranger clasps a stranger's hand,
  Their trust is great to see,
To open the door to a peaceful land
  Love is the golden key!
                    — Jessie Cannon Elridge

Express Love

Lastly, pray that God will enable you to love those who arouse bitter and hateful thoughts and attitudes in your mind and soul. Then act as if you did love. Treat your husband as you did when you were sweethearts. Tell him that you love him. Tell your stubborn daughter how attractively she fixes the salad. Tell your son that you appreciate the way he accepts responsibility in delivering the newspapers each morning. Tell your nosey neighbor that she does have the prettiest flower arrangement. Compliment the soloist at church Sunday.

We tend to forget that to love is a commandment. God commands, "Love one another." And He did not amend it with, "That is, if you feel like it." And besides, love is an act of the will. Someone has said, "Love is not a feeling to be felt, but an acting to be learned." It's also true that when in obedience to God we show love by our actions, feeling inevitably follows.

As you walk this love-road the end is God, the source and ultimate object of all love. You don't walk alone, for He'll go with you hand in hand.

You just can't afford to hate!

16

Faith for Today

Where does faith in God — believing the unseen — come into the economic security of today?

We no longer need to pray, "Give us today's meal." We see to that! Our shelves are full, the freezer loaded, and according to the budget the week's salary will adequately cover the necessities. Or, we can buy on time.

We carry accident and fire insurance. We pay into Social Security, which guarantees help when old age limits our capacity to earn. Is there a place for faith in these advanced stages of medical discoveries and techniques? When fatal diseases of fifty years ago are practically conquered? When failure of the heart to beat does not mean sure death? When surgical skills and wonder drugs perform miracles?

How about faith and today's intellectual level? We're educated and have learned facts of science, economics, life, or behaviorism. The conclusion is simple — follow such-and-such procedure and the result is certain. Of course, there's an element of truth wrapped up in this. The Bible says, "Whatsoever a man soweth, that shall he also reap" (Gal. 6:7). We know if you sow a grain of wheat, you'll harvest wheat. But in this age of logic and reason, of calculations and deductions, of do-it-yourself kits, is there room for faith in determining what to do, where to live, or in solving your personal problems? Room for faith in One who dares to operate beyond and above the known?

Have we advanced beyond the practical side of faith? Is it a mere theory stuck away in a remote, dusty part of the mind of old fogies?

Without Faith

All the economic, intellectual, and professional attainments dare not be separated from their Originator — God. To take faith in Him out of today's culture and living we have only a framework, a shell. We then give honor to the creature and his accomplishments rather than to the Creator of all intellect, of all materials.

The lack of faith amid today's culture produces insecurity, fear, and tension. Even with our so-called security and logical conclusions and reasoning, many problems, conflicts, and disappointments still exist. In times like these, without faith in an all-wise God, individuals become frustrated and panicky. They resort to sedatives or to pleasure, become escapists, turn neurotic, or may even take life. Their balloon has burst. They can't put it together again.

What Is Faith?

Let's think about a mother's personal faith — believing the unseen, having confidence in the unknown.

William Newton Clarke says, "Faith is the daring of the soul to go farther than it can see."[1] According to

A.B. Evans, "Faith is not a sense, nor sight, nor reason, but taking God at His word."[2]

Yes, faith is "being convinced of things not seen." But as we take the step of faith the mist is lifted, the hidden suddenly becomes known.

It reminds me of the electrically controlled doors seen at many places of business. You can step close, stop, reach out your hand, and push with all your might, but the door doesn't budge. However, if you just keep walking on as though the door were open, it opens and you step right into the store. Faith goes ahead. It doesn't stop and wait till everything is clear.

Faith in the Homemaker's Life

Yes, indeed, faith should play an important part in a homemaker's life. In major catastrophes — crop failure, loss of job, death, illness, accident, injury, moving time — she can take hold of God's hand and find His supreme will and His presence.

Just now there flashes into my mind that terrific storm at sea; the airplane ride with one engine feathered; the overturned car; the serious illness with my husband away from home; "face to face" with death! Faith in God carried me through each incident! Faith in God's words, "I will **never** leave thee, nor forsake thee" (Heb. 13:5). "All things work together for good to them that **love** God" (Rom. 8:28).

Faith replaces worry, the anxious thoughts concerning necessities. We all know worry never changed an inch of our growth, and it hasn't given anything but gray hairs and troubles. Remember the motto that reads: "If you trust, you do not worry. If you worry, you do not trust."

Even in the daily necessities the homemaker with eyes of faith sees God who promised, "So don't worry and don't keep saying, 'What shall we eat, what shall we drink, or what shall we wear?' . . . your Heavenly Father knows that you need them all. Set your heart on his kingdom and his goodness, and all these things will come to you as a matter of course" (Matt. 6:31-33;Phillips).

But remember, God hasn't promised to supply our wants, just our needs. Frankly, this is where I think the majority of us get bogged down. We center far too much time, energy, and anxious thought around our wants. The lure of an abundance of nice, attractive, and enjoyable things often dims our common sense and needs.

We need faith to give calmness when our children leave us just to attend school. Faith that God will protect them from injury or evil, faith that no impure attitude or habit will fix its gripping claws like a scorpion into their character. We need faith in God that He'll protect on the highway, in our travels, and even in our homes, as we think of accidents, plane crashes, and maniacs' caprices. We need faith that God will heal, even if we have access to skilled medical care and miracle drugs. In our home, God has honored our faith many times. I'm thinking now of the time pneumonia was ready to claim our two year old; when a clot darted hither and yon in my bloodstream after our daughter's birth.

We need to have faith that God will help our children to accept Him, to accept truth, and to enfold it into their philosophy of life, thoughts, and acts. We need to have faith that they will place their wills and lives into God's hands and let Him control them. Our faith, our beliefs, will never serve as proxy for theirs. Our children must personally accept God through Jesus Christ and then make His ideas and wishes their own. Yet our acts and prayers of faith somehow do affect their lives.

Faith Is Based on Truth

Faith is an atmosphere in which we live and more. It is an absolute necessity, even in twentieth century living.

Faith is not a supernatural charge or feeling. It is a conscious knowledge of "God has said," and therefore it is true because His words **never** change, regardless of feelings or circumstances. We see the unseen, we know of a certainty, because through the eyes of faith we see God and His eternal truths.

I'm thinking just now of an occasion when God showed me in a new way that faith is not a feeling and does not belong to the subconscious stratum. It belongs to our conscious thinking. After being away from home (traveling two nights on the train), I returned to my family. My hired help was ill, schools were closed due to the heaviest snow of the year, and the house was disorderly. Work had piled up in the office and a radio script was due! I sat down, weary of body and mind, thinking, *I can't. I don't know where to begin!* Then the Spirit spoke: "But my God shall supply **all** your needs" (Phil. 4:19).

In desperation I began explaining every detail to God, and soon concluded, "God, I'm weary and frustrated. I need wisdom to know what to do first and what to write. I need physical strength, I need courage, I need to forget all that I can't get done today." And you know, I pitched right in, conscious that God was helping.

"But," someone says, "I've been praying and praying and trying to have this kind of faith." It is not a reward of works. Faith is a gift from the heart of God.

Faith "can only come from hearing the message, and the message is the Word of Christ." Faith is based on knowing the truth.

So, faith is a by-product of knowing God's words. These you find in the Bible. Also, as you read about the lives of others who applied God's truths, and as you associate with those who possess great faith, your own faith will be strengthened and increased.

Passing on Faith to Our Children

Someone has said, "If for any reason whatever a child be taught but one lesson, let that lesson be faith in God. For that one step towards an education is of more permanent value than all other learning put together."

The most important lesson for our children today is faith. Not faith in our economic security. Not faith in intellectual attainment. Not faith in man or man's achievement, but:

> Faith in God — who knows everything, who sees everything.
>
> Faith in God — who has all power. "With God, nothing is impossible."
>
> Faith in God — who because of Jesus Christ, can forgive sin and restore whoever comes to Him into harmonious, perfect relationship with Him.
>
> Faith in God — who alone can lift today's humanity from wallowing in the mud of immorality.
>
> Faith in God — who is Sovereign, the One who ultimately controls individuals, authorities, and nations.

You know, we can't give to another that which we do not possess ourselves. If we wish to help our child possess such a faith we first must have this faith to share.

From such an atmosphere our children will unconsciously absorb faith as they do oxygen from the natural air. Even the young ones will acquire some of it before they are old enough to understand intellectually. Teach your child faith!

Remember, to successfully meet life's situations in a changing world you need faith in the eternal God.

NOTES

Chapter 1
[1]Dorothy Haskin, "Job for a Queen," *Moody Monthly* (August, 1958).
[2]Florida Scott-Maxwell, "The Greatness of the Task," *Ladies' Home Journal*.
[3]Dr. John Bowlby, *Ladies' Home Journal* (November, 1958), p. 154.
[4]Ibid.

Chapter 2
[1]Clyde M. Narramore, *Happiness in Marriage* (Grand Rapids, MI; Zondervan, 1961), p.5.

Chapter 3
[1]*The Christian Leader's Golden Treasury* (Indianapolis, IN: Groffell & Dunlap, 1955), p. 610.
[2]Ibid., p. 608.
[3]Charles M. Crowe as cited in *ibid.*

Chapter 4
[1]*Power for Living* (Wheaton, IL: Scripture Press).
[2]David R. Mace, *Success in Marriage* (Nashville, TN: Abingdon).

Chapter 6
[1]Some of the ideas expressed in this chapter are taken from Clyde M. Narramore, *How to Handle Fear, This Way to Happiness* (Grand Rapids, MI: Zondervan, 1958).

Chapter 7
[1]Helen Gibson Hogue, *The Christian Home* (Nashville, TN: Board of Education, The Methodist Church).

Chapter 8
[1]*Newsweek* — Winter-Spring 1990, "The 21st Century Family."
[2]Ibid., — April 2, 1990.

Chapter 10

[1] David R. Mace, *Success in Marriage* (Nashville, TN: Abingdon, n.d.).

[2] Phyllis C. Michael, *Poems for Mothers* (Grand Rapids, MI: Zondervan, 1963), Used by permission.

Chapter 11

[1] *The Christian Leader's Golden Treasury* (Indianapolis, IN: Groffell & Dunlap, 1955), p. 101-102.

[2] Ibid., p. 102.

Chapter 12

[1] Vance Havner, *Pleasant Paths* (Old Tappan, NY: Fleming H. Revell Co., 1945).

[2] Ibid.

Chapter 14

[1] Sven Stolpe, *Dag Hammarskjöld: A Spiritual Portrait* (New York, NY: Charles Scribner's Sons, 1966).

Chapter 15

[1] Clarence E. Macartney, *Macartney's Illustrations* (Nashville, TN: Abingdon Press, n.d.), p. 154.

[2] *Christian Leaders Golden Treasury* (Indianapolis, IN: Groffell & Dunlap, 1955), p. 256

Chapter 16

[1] Ibid., p. 181.

[2] Ibid., p. 176.